BORDERTOWN
MEMORIES

THIS IS A TRUE STORY

[signature]

JUAN MEDINA

ISBN: 978-1-957203-20-1 (sc)
ISBN: 978-1-957203-21-8 (hc)
ISBN: 978-1-957203-22-5 (e)

THE EWINGS
PUBLISHING

One Galleria Blvd., Suite 1900, Metairie, LA 70001
1-888-421-2397

CONTENTS

Sidro Vatos, from right to left; Clarence Arroyo (RIP) George Miranda, author, Ralph Lopez, Juan (Guero) Michaels, Carlos Mercado, circa 1977, picture courtesy of Carmen Vasquez

AN INTRODUCTION: NEVER KILLED ANYONE NEVER HAD ANYONE KILLED

**Corruption and betrayal.
Lust and heartbreak. Drugs and murder.**

This is a true account during a period of this writer's life that was met with deep regret and sorrow.

It is the story of the life of a drug dealer beginning in the late 1960s through the late '70s in my beloved town of San Ysidro. During that period marijuana and cocaine deals were made by the ton loads and should not be compared to the drug busts that customs agents and other law enforcement officials would see during their career in the '80s and beyond.

By 2011 the then sleepy little town "Barrio Sidro" located along the border to Mexico, had grown into the largest border crossing in the world. With 70,000 northbound vehicles, and 20,000 northbound pedestrians crossing daily.[1] It's this writer's opinion that very activity spawned what are now the major drug cartels in Mexico and Latin America.

By the mid '70s, drugs were being delivered by the ton in shipments to San Ysidro drug dealers and with-it incredible amounts of cash were flowing back into Mexico via Tijuana to pay off the Mexican drug dealers. During that period the term "drug cartels" did not yet exist, but over time more people from Culiacan, Sinaloa and Guadalajara, Jalisco began setting up shop in Tijuana, attracted by the easy cash. The drug dealing climate began to radically change.

---

[1] Reuters June 22, 2011

In a book by Joseph Wambaugh, titled *"Lines and Shadows"* the author writes about an original task force put together to fight the lawlessness occurring along the hills of the border, also known as "the imaginary line" between San Ysidro and Tijuana. The Border Alien Robbery Force (BARF) was responsible for clearing up crime along the southern border of San Ysidro and of the eastern regions."[2] What Mr. Wambaugh does not mention is any action against drug runners, who were also using these routes through the hills in San Ysidro. So, I asked a childhood friend, retired from a career as a Custom's Official, that same question.

> *"I can do better than that; I get you an interview with someone who was in the BARF squad!"*

My friend sets up the meeting at a local restaurant. The following is an excerpt of that conversation.

"He asked me why Joe Wambaugh had not mentioned anything about drugs in his book "Lines and Shadows" and my reply was simply that both Customs Patrol and Border Patrol had no intelligence or information on drug smuggling and drug information and intel was not shared by other agencies such as the DEA and other law enforcement agencies. I asserted that the seizure of drugs had more to do with simply running into the smugglers back in the '70s. In those days drugs were backpacked through the foothills of Otay Mountains and Pio Pico was used as a beacon where the duffel bags where hidden along Telegraph Canyon Road. Later the drugs were picked up by someone who would throw the duffel bags into his car and drive out of the area. The backpackers used trails that were east of Johnnie Wolf's place (Wolf's place was located just north of where the Otay Mesa Port of Entry is today). There were areas along the border where the smugglers simply drove their vehicles loaded with dope across the border. Either there was no fence, or they simply cut through the fence. On the west side of the San Ysidro POE (Port of Entry) the vehicles entered through Smugglers Canyon, Spooner's Mesa and Goat Canyon. On the east side of the San Ysidro POE the vehicles entered through many areas such as Wruck Canyon, which had an array of dirt roads that eventually allowed one to drive from the border all the way

---

[2] Lines and Shadows, by Joseph Wambaugh copyright 1982

up to Otay Mesa Road and Dillion Trail. One favorite spot for the smugglers was between the soccer field and "Washer Woman Flats." Another favorite spot for drive throughs was the southern end of Cactus Road. Not many loads were brought through the ocean/coast because of the Coast Guard vigilance. I also mentioned that most of the drugs were being smuggled at the POE's with the assistance of corrupt INS or customs inspectors. I failed to mention that there were also corrupt customs inspectors at commercial warehouses, of the area that were on drug cartel payroll. I also failed to mention that bikers on dirt bikes also smuggled duffel bags of dope right through Wruck Canyon. The bikers would cross Otay Mesa Road north and take their duffel bags into the Otay River area where they would offload at Colonia Del Boo (El Barrio de Otay) in Otay Valley. Everybody was aware of what was going on, but we simply did not have the manpower to cover such areas. Sometimes we had less than one dozen agents per shift and we had to cover the area from the border park south of Imperial Beach all the way to Dulzura! Frankly, drug smuggling and addressing corruption were not considered a priority for the U.S. government in the '70s. Or perhaps the big boys at the Potomac wanted it that way. Quien sabe! (Who knows?)

That said there was no doubt in my mind that by 1989 the drug cartels had some of the Headquarters Customs Internal Affairs and Customs Office of Investigations top managers on their payroll!

Another question he asked me was about when Customs Internal Affairs sent me to work in D.C., then while I was gone shut down an investigation, I was working on regarding a corruption case involving half a dozen inspectors at the Calexico POE had been memorialized. My answer was simply that I had furnished the info to the FBI and the Treasury I.G. and that they along with the Customs Service had simply circled-the-wagons against me. In other words, they covered it up.

However, when I got home, I did recall that in 1992 the federal government did publish a book dubbed, "Serious Mismanagement and Misconduct in the Treasury Department, Customs Service, and Other Federal Agencies and The Adequacy of Efforts To Hold Agency Officials Accountable." The information in the book was the result of the hearings before the Commerce, Consumer, and Monetary Affairs Subcommittee of the Committee on

Government Operations and House of Representatives. On page 1505 it was annotated that the Treasury I.G. investigator was ordered to close my allegations administratively and the investigator's file folder was taken away in its entirety. On page 1506 it is annotated that the I.G. investigator was told by her supervisor, Ralph Garcia that "Charles" (The Assistant Treasury I.G. at that time was Charles Fowler and the IG was Donald Kirkendall), wanted the case closed and that's what they were going to do! Major coverup and none of the three (Garcia, Fowler and Kirkendall) were ever held accountable!

In substance, what I am asserting is that I agree with your friend that proliferation of drug smuggling may have begun here in the San Ysidro and Tijuana area. After all, Tijuana was the bastion for the movement and availability of illegal drugs, bordellos, gambling, horseracing, rooster fights and a rest stop for the Pollos headed north. Pero at the same time I think that our own government were the enablers for illegal drugs because IA management made it almost impossible for us to work the corruption cases that involved corrupt customs employees. When I was detailed to go to D.C. to pull files and stuff envelopes in the basement, I knew it was time to leave IA."[3]

I also asked him why he isn't mentioned in the book.

> *"Because I did not want to be interviewed by Joe (Wambaugh), I did not socialize with those guys from the PD, I did not drink or smoke, which did not fit well either, and you have to remember that I was with the Custom's squad that made up the team, after each shift I would simply go home."*

The meeting went very well, supplying a lot of information for this book. And I couldn't help but find it ironic that here you have an ex-drug dealer interviewing two ex-customs officials! That evening at dinner my friend is waving his finger at me, *"You must know that we did have our radar on you, we were just too busy chasing down our own people and let you go ahead. You were very lucky indeed that we did not catch up to you!"*

---

[3] Richard Medina, former U. S. Customs Official

If it weren't for the socio-political Chicano Movement of the '60s things could have gone all wrong. Prison and even death were at arm's length but through this opportunity I managed to survive.

For my participation in the Chicano Movement, I was nominated and selected as an Undergraduate Fellow at California State University, Sacrament. Looking back at everything I saw and all I experienced I know I was lucky. Not only did I come out of this period of my life alive, but somehow without an arrest record. The program began in the fall term of September 1969. There was no better time to get out of San Ysidro. One of my biggest regrets is not graduating with my degree and even ignoring a scholarship offer for a master's program at Stanford University, why? Because I was making too much money for my own good, by the early 70's my life turned into what I foolishly aspired to be, a "Superfly" The movie inspired me in the worst way.

I've decided to share my experiences with readers in the hope of warning those who are considering entering into a life of drugs and crime to be aware of the consequences. Many of my childhood friends were not as lucky as I was. Together we faced the same socio-economic disadvantages that plague all southern border towns; including high poverty rates, unemployment, crime-infested barrios, discrimination and racism and low-achieving schools, among other things. From San Ysidro to Brownsville, Texas, the same penalties play out for those lured into drug dealing by the grandeur sex, money and power: violent death, long prison terms, drug addiction, broken marriages and dysfunctional families.

It's also because of my experiences that I believe there is no better method for cleaning up one's karma than helping others in need. So, after 1989 I devoted my life to doing just that—helping young heroin addicts change their ways and ultimately enter the workforce as productive citizens. I thank God for giving me a good sense of judgment. I never killed anyone or ordered anyone to be killed. Had I done so it's likely I would not be alive to write this book today.

Northbound traffic into San Ysidro, Circa 1959

1

THE BORDERTOWN MEMORIES

n the summer of 1957 the family moved into the house at 106 East Park in San Ysidro, coming from Calexico it was almost a four-hour ride west. In 1960 the U.S Census reports the population of San Ysidro as 4,860 with 2,512 inhabitants of Spanish surnames, with more than half of the population being Mexican. Latinos were not identified but rather counted as "White." In addition, the census does not identify African-Americans or Asians living in San Ysidro.

I asked a friend about this who is a former chairperson of the San Ysidro Planning Commission.

"One difficulty in establishing population by census is that the community boundaries changed and so did the census tracts," he said. "In some cases, I had to extrapolate the numbers, trying to match up census maps of yesteryear to current ones. They never matched entirely."[4]

He's 8 years old when his mom decides to take her kids to follow the man she calls his father. Mom, at 25 years old is very beautiful, strong-willed and a hard worker. As a boy he recalls her working the fields of Visalia, picking

---

[4] September 9, 2018, Michael Freedman, Chairperson of the San Ysidro Planning Commission, former Community Development Manager at Casa Familiar, a San Ysidro non-profit Community-based Organization.

dates in Indio, Calif. The boy's memory of his father is fuzzy since he was always away from home. She has four kids now, the eldest of who had just turned 8, that May, sister Chacha turned 7, brother Tury 5 and little sister Petunia was going on 3. Soon after coming to San Ysidro, the kids become aware of the problems their parents were having. Mom is more stressed than before, making the kids more aware that something was wrong. Their father was away more often and when he did come home the kids witnessed the fighting, beatings; and soon mom discovers her husband had children with another woman! Around this time the eldest boy is stricken with rheumatic fever, which leaves him practically crippled. Suffering from the pain and torment of not being able to walk he also begins to learn of the serious problems the family is having.

One night he was lying in bed with all his siblings asleep in the same room. Suddenly he hears loud voices, screaming, banging, slapping, then he hears his mom crying while his father screams insults at her. Something very bad is happening to his mother. He tries to get up, but his legs won't move the way he wants them to. His whole lower body hurts badly. He edge's himself out of bed, falls on the floor and uses his arms to drag his body to his parent's room. He sees his mom half naked, bleeding from her face, the palm of her hand with a big, bloody gash where she tried to protect herself from being split open with an old pointed can opener. The boy screams as loud as he can, and they turn. His father runs out of the room and leaves the house.

In the morning mom goes to Dr. Bajo's office to get her cuts treated the boy follows her with a crutch that the owner of a local second-hand store gave mom to help him walk. The man named Chester would flirt with mom and give her stuff for free to get in good with her. At the doctor's office, Dr. Bajo begins his treatment for the rheumatic fever the boy is suffering from. After many visits to Dr. Bajo's office things begin to normalize, and the boy's rheumatic fever episodes and pain begin to fade. Soon the boy can walk again and the household stress begins to fade. Mom starts divorce proceedings with the help of her attorney and the kids are ready to start school that fall.

Across the street from the house was the library on San Ysidro Blvd. This is where he saw some guys frequently hanging out and you wanted to see what they are doing. They are much older than him but that didn't deter him. One day he ventures across the street to hang out. You hear names like Paco, Arturo, Kiki, Carlos, Jaime, Joe and others. After the second or third day the guys notice "the new kid" hanging around. They go over to him and ask all sorts of questions. He answers the best he can and points across the street to where he lives. *"OK, so you want to hang out with us? Let's go to the alley."* He follows not realizing what's going on. They form a circle around him and begin yelling, and then they push him into a circle where a chubby, blonde-haired, with a cowlick right above his forehead, the kid is about his age. They're expecting a fight! The kid looks mean and he comes at him, so they grapple to the ground, but don't really hurt each other. The older guys get bored and walk away, leaving them in the dirt of the alley. The boys get up and slap the dirt off their clothes. The chubby kid is looking at him, and suddenly to his surprise, he says *"Wanna go play?"* *"I guess so"* he replies.

After that he and Georgie become the best of friends. Georgie would show him all that San Ysidro had to offer a young kid. The boy comes to love San Ysidro, especially playing in "the hills," that magical place northeast of San Ysidro where there were no houses. They would run around playing cowboys and Indians, sliding down "Clay Hill" on a piece of cardboard and sneaking up to the dump to see what they could take. The watchman would chase the boys off most of the time but they did manage to take stuff like bike parts, girlie magazines, and one time they found a big bag of firecrackers that the customs officials at the border confiscated and dumped there.

Here in his own little piece of paradise he would not know that in a little more than a decade it would become what Joseph Wambaugh in 1984 describes in his book **Lines and Shadows**.

> *"Now in a zone of only a few square miles, in effect a no-man's land between the cities of Tijuana, Mexico and San Diego, USA they came. Sometimes ten thousand per week. And in those canyons lurked Tijuana bandits and cutthroats who fed off the pollos (the*

term used for undocumented immigrants heading north as they crossed the frontier in the night. One of the slashes of earth in this no-man's land is called Deadman's Canyon for good reason. It is a mean, blood-drenched gash of mesquite and cactus and rocks within the city limits of San Diego."

One evening a Lieutenant wrote a strange acronym on their chalkboard. It read B.A.R.F. When asked what it meant the Lieutenant said, "Border Alien Robbery Force."[5]

The Mexican-American cops who formed the BARF, (who also called themselves "the gunslingers") interacted with the *"Vatos de Sidro"* as all the kids from San Ysidro would proudly call themselves. One cop who was white became well known and liked by the vatos. They called him *"El Jura de Sidro"* (The cop from Sidro, Sgt. Kelly). Once it was known how easy it was to cross these hills and what Wambaugh described as the *"the imaginary line between two cities, two countries, two economies…"* the drug-runners appeared, lugging duffel bags of marijuana to sell to the local drug dealers and beyond. Later he remembered these were the same places that he and his friends would play and explore with so much wonder, freedom and fun.

The most important thing to him was that now he is one of the *Vatos de Sidro.* He will never forget that very special first summer in Sidro! He is now a member of "mi barrio Sidro!" It seems to him that everyone needs to identify with something and the vatos he hung out with were no different. In junior high they gave themselves names like The Romans and later in high school their group would call themselves The Bootleggers. They didn't think of themselves as a gang, just a name to identify themselves with, something to belong to.

As school starts in the fall of 1957, he's enrolled into Mrs. Smith's fourth grade class at Beyer Elementary School. He's thrilled about the new school, making more friends than he ever did in Calexico.

---

[5] Lines and Shadows, Joseph Wambaugh, 1984

To *"start the new school-year right"* Mrs. Smith says, *"We will begin by changing a few names. Roberto, you will be Robert now; Ricardo, you will be Richard; Rodolfo, you will be Rudy, and Juan you will be John.*

He was excited about getting a new name. John like the macho man himself, John Wayne! He can't wait to get home and tell the whole family about his new name.

Soon he gets his social security card with his new name and at 16 years old, his new driver's license. When he registers for the U.S. draft his name is also John. He makes sure that no one will take his new name away. Later, as he embraces the Chicano Movement with a now different worldview, he realizes what a mistake it was to change his name from Juan to John. He is now more politically aware and realizes that his film hero went around killing Indians and Mexicans and was nothing more than another white conquistador. The "cowboys and Indians" movies he saw were just perpetuating the white man's culture of killing off people of color. That's the reason why in just a few years he would come to regret letting Mrs. Smith change his name. He still thinks of her with high regards because she was a very good teacher; she loved history and made every effort to encourage her students to love history as well. Early California history became his favorite subject with specific interest in friars setting up missions along the California coast to bring Christianity to the Indians. That part of the country that would later be called San Diego. Mrs. Smith was also admired in the community for her involvement in community affairs and for the well-being of her students. He loved Mrs. Smith for all the work he saw her do for her students.

In a couple of years, he's enrolled into The San Ysidro Little League and assigned to a team called "The Tigers." One of his childhood heroes ended up being his very first coach Emil. Everyone just called him Emo and he was an inspiration to the whole team, which after a win would be treated to cherry cokes at Soto's pharmacy; perhaps the oldest soda fountain in San Diego County.

His generosity continued off the field too. Somehow Emo managed to take
the whole team to Jack Murphy Stadium to watch the San Diego Padres
play. He would also take the team to his house for carne asada prepared by
his wife Virginia, who became like a second mom to the team. The boy who
is still suffering from rheumatic fever episodes at this time is so proud to
wear the team uniform even though he's most often sitting on the bench.

With the help of Georgie, who was also the team's catcher, San Ysidro
becomes his wonderland. Riding his bike up and down the Boulevard, he
had always been fascinated by the fire station, which was just a couple of
doors up from Dr. Bajo's office. Since he doesn't recall ever seeing a fire
in San Ysidro, he's often wonder what those guys do all day long. During
a stop one day in front of the firehouse he's just hanging out on his bike,
with one foot on the ground and the next resting on the front bar. Soon the
fire men come out with a couple of stools to sit on and appear to just wait,
frequently looking to the corner of Cottonwood Road. In a few minutes it
becomes clear what they're waiting for. Coming around the corner are two
beautiful girls in their mid-teens wearing short shorts. As they walk by Dr.
Bajo's office he can see the girls are identical. They giggle as they pass by
and he is wide-eyed and open mouthed. When the girls get in front of the
fire house one of them kind of waves with her little finger to the guys and
as they reach the boy on his bike the girl nearest pushes him hard enough
to land him ass-first on top of his bike. As they continue on their path, he
has a view from a different angle with his butt on the sidewalk. Then all of
a sudden, he hears hollering and knee-slapping laughter coming from the
fire house. The fire guys are having a real fun time watching everything
play out. One of the fire men still laughing comes over and helps him get up.

> *"Son, you have just been introduced to the Baker twins. Come on in,
> you hungry? Want a coke?"*

"Well OK."

The guy gives him a sandwich and a coke, telling him that the Baker twins
usually walk by the fire house around this time almost every day.

"They kind of just flirt with us when they walk by on most days, and we certainly don't mind it. Pretty aren't they?"

"Well yeah."

The man shows him around the fire house and the boy is in awe.

Because most parents couldn't afford the price of a bike in a store, kids were forced to piece them together from here and there, even from the dump in the hills in the alley behind Georgie's house. All the kids had bikes built like this. He and the boys covered a lot of ground, not only San Ysidro but all along Monument Road, Hollister Street, Nestor, Palm City, Imperial Beach and the Silver Strand. The Sidro vatos loved the challenge of traveling distances into other barrios. One challenge was getting to the Vogue Theater in Chula Vista, which was about nine miles from the starting point at George's. The challenge was not only the distance, but also getting through the four blocks of Otay from Main Street to Anita Street, without catching the attention of the rival Otay barrio vatos catching them in their territory. In order to catch a movie, the Sidro boys would start out early in the morning to get to the matinee on time. The boys are at full speed down Beyer Blvd. past the Silver Wing at the top of the Otay Mesa, the area now crammed with huge housing tracts and strip malls. The beautiful Otay River Valley spreads out below. Coming down the hill they begin to gain speed and start hollering, allowing those little bikes to go as fast as they can. They reach Main Street and pedal hard to get past Anita Street. At this point they still have about five miles to go but they are celebrating it as a victory. At the Vogue they throw the bikes at the side of the building since no one would ever bother with them. At the end of the show, it is back to Sidro!

2

POP SEES MOM

The big man is sitting at Jim's Café with his boss Bill Merrick (he calls him Willy). Willy is a horse trainer and ranch owner. They're at their usual seat where the window faces east toward the boulevard, they are having breakfast after finishing their morning chores when the big man spots her coming out of Duran's Market.

"Wow, new girl in town." She is walking west *toward "la botica"* or Soto's Pharmacy. He drops his fork and tells Willy, "I'll be back in a bit." Willy sees what he is after and smiles. The big man runs out to cross the street.

He later he tells the kid about how it all came through for him and the kid's mom, and the kid imagines the big man running after her with his tail wagging like a street dog. He says how hard it was to convince his mom to go out with him, but he did and the rest was history.

Mom tells her son later what she thinks of him.

> "Esta Grandote, Prieto, y Feo, pero lo quiero mucho!"
> (He is big, too brown and ugly, but I love him a lot).

The big man with a big smile loves San Ysidro and San Ysidro loved him. He stood at 6 feet 2 inches and weighed about 220 pounds. On one of his first visits to the boy's house the big man pulls up in a 1958 model 88 Oldsmobile with a white convertible top, gray and white body, big white-wall tires and shiny chrome tear-drop flood light lamps. He takes the family for an afternoon cruise and the kid got to ride shotgun while mom was in the center next to him. The big man drives up to Silver Wing hill where you can see all the way to the ocean, south to the hills of Tijuana. The "Wing" is a monument to the early aviators that would try out their homemade machines with ideas to fly. The kid is in total awe of the big man—from the way he walks to singing Mexican songs with mom. He had never met someone like that before.

He is a Korean War veteran and was a boxer in the Army. He tells the kid a story of how some guys jumped him once after a fight because he wouldn't intentionally lose. *"They kicked my balls in pretty bad,"* he tells the kid, adding the doctor said he probably wouldn't be able to father any more children. That information was dispelled after he had three more kids with mom. Not only was he strong, but quick on his feet. One day at the racetrack the big man was timing a horse for the usual morning workout and as the horse and jockey come around the turn the horse hits the railing and both jockey and horse go down. The boy watched as the big man ran like a bullet train toward the accident, got the jockey up, and then practically lifts the horse to its feet. Willy pats him on the back and says, *"Joe that was something else what you just did."* To the boy it was reminiscent of Superman. Another time the kid saw a mare being bred by a stallion, a scene he would never forget. The kid is inside a tall round pen maybe 20 to 25 feet in diameter. The stallion is jumping, bucking, neighing and snorting like he knows what's going to happen. The mare is brought into the pen and the stallion becomes more excited. The mare is comforted by another ranch hand by caressing her face and nose. The big man walks up to the excited stallion and murmurs to the horse, *"Easy, easy mijo, that's a good boy."*

He puts a rope around the horse's neck. As he gets the horse close to the mares behind, he grabs the mare's tail. The kid is thinking about how easily she could back kick him and he would be in a world of hurt. Then the kid realizes that somehow both he and the mare know she won't kick, and she doesn't. What happens next leaves the kid in awe. The stallion is led to the mare's behind and the front hoofs of the big horse rise to straddle her hips.

Sweat from the big man's forearms was glistening in the sun. Then the big man drops the rope and with his left hand guides the stallions' enormous penis into the mares' behind. The size of that penis was about a wide around as the big man's forearm and just about as long! At 10 years old the scene he had witnessed made him feel proud of the big man. Breeding didn't take long, maybe two minutes at the most and that was it. Both horses, unharmed and satisfied, are led back to their respective corrals.

The big man loved motorcycles and belonged to a club called "Los Jorongos MC." A Jorongo is a Mexican vest made from thick colored wool with red, white, green and blue. It had the club insignia sewn to the back of the vest with one's moniker in front. His moniker was "Pepe le Pieu" the lover-boy cartoon skunk from Looney-Tunes. The big man would take the boy everywhere. In the morning he would ride the motor bike with the kid in the back to the ranch, jump on a horse for the morning workout, and then get on a tractor to rake the track, feed the horses and then off to his other job as a house-mover driving a big-rig. Next it would back to the ranch for the afternoon feeding where he taught the kid how to properly clean the corrals and stables. Finally, late in the afternoon it was back home.

3

WILLY'S RANCH

Willy's ranch was located on a street *that is* no longer there today. From the ranch to the north you could see Southwest Jr. High School, the school he would attend in a few years. Directly to the south was the Tijuana River Valley (or the "River Bottom" as the area was called). Beyond it are the hills of Tijuana and about two miles to the west was the ocean. In this valley there were colorful fields of tomatoes, asparagus and strawberries. He loved the view from all directions of the ranch and if it wasn't for Highway 101, now Interstate 5, he could imagine it a place seen in the movies where the cowboys and Indians would fight. It was here where he learned how to ride a horse, warming them up for their final workout in the mornings. For him the ranch was a magical place. This is where he learned how to drive a tractor, which was so much fun but also made him feel important. Every three months or so, he would have to spread manure around the inside of the track with the tractor rake and then blend it into the soil. That area of the field was so rich and fertile that anything could have grown there, but the real cash crop were the horses.

Willy's ranch held horses in transit from the race track and then back to their home ranch. Willy's ranch rented out stables and corrals to owners, so their horses could spend the night or, sometimes for weeks while prepping for a race at the Agua Caliente race track in Tijuana. There were always horses at the ranch for different reasons. The big man would do it all from shoeing to veterinary needs and breeding. The kid remembers the time the big man was called out to the ranch because none of the handlers could get a newly arrived horse unloaded from the van because it was too nervous. Its nighttime but the kid asks if he can tag along. He watches intently as the big man walks into the van speaking softly to the horse.

> *"Come on mijo, stop all this stuff, and let's go out so you can get something to eat, eh?"*

When the horse walks down the plank away from the van everyone shook their heads in disbelief. The big man's fame for calming hard to handle horses grew in San Ysidro and beyond. A "horse whisperer" they call them today. Yeah, the big man was one of those.

The kid is so impressed and proud to be with the big man that he soon begins calling him "Pop" and he instructs his sisters and brother to do the same. Pop soon marries mom and is now part of the family. Word soon gets out and now the whole town is now calling him Pop.

You could find Pop daily at any one of his favorite hangouts. From Jim's Café to Mr. Cuens' San Ysidro Feed and Grain, to the Paddock bar, you never saw him drink or smoke. Pop would go to the Paddock bar just to catch up with race track guys and see who's betting on what horse at any given time. That big smile of his was all up and down the boulevard.

Then there was Maistro's Pool Hall, which was small and only had two tables; the front for playing 9 and 8-ball and the one in the back for Snooker and Golf. When Pop played pool (on the back table) it would always be with Arturo or Johnny because no one else was good enough to play with him for even a few bucks. When the game was on the word quickly got out and Maistro's pool hall would fill with spectators. These guys were the best in town and there was sure to be a show of skill, and entertainment. Pop literally danced around the pool table. Whenever he made an amazing shot and the oohs and ahs began, he would start up with his jitterbug moves. He loved the jitterbug. He would dance with the cue stick, making his opponents even more edgy.

Being Pop's kid had special privileges at Maistro's Pool Hall because whenever Pop played pool more paying customers would come in and Maistro himself would allow the underage boy to come inside. He took a liking to the kid and after asking Maistro if he could do some chores for him around the pool hall, he got the job of brushing down the tables, sweeping and taking out the trash. But most important to him was that during off hours and after completing his chores, Maistro would allow him to practice playing pool! The kid is not quite tall enough yet to set up a good pool shooting stance, but he tries. He gets to love the game and slowly gets better. Later as an adult he would ask Pop to accompany him to pool tournaments at various bars with pool tables all over Chula Vista. He and Pop entered doubles Eight Ball tournaments and always came home with a trophy. He soon had his own mantel filled with Pool Tournament trophies.

THE HORSE RANCHES OF SAN YSIDRO

I n the early years San Ysidro was home to many horse ranches, adding to the local economy and feeding the gambling need for many at the Agua Caliente race track in Tijuana. Being a native of San Ysidro Pop knew all the ranchers in town. One of his jobs was to transport horses to the race track and back to ranches, near and far, sometimes across the country.

He always had the "kid" with him, or as he told his friends "the ol' lady's kid." By the time the kid could push a wheelbarrow through the sand in the horse corrals Pop would get him a job at one of the local ranches. There was always a ranch to work at. Summers were for working the horse ranches Five bucks a day for cleaning corrals and depending on the size of the ranch there could be between eight and 12 horse stables and corrals per day. It was hard work for a skinny kid to push a wheelbarrow full of horse manure through sand, sun and sometimes some threatening thoroughbred horses that are as feisty as they are beautiful. But he held his ground and got the job done. Pop taught him how to calm a horse down by rubbing a rake up and down their backs. The horses loved that.

It was at the Leadman Ranch where the kid's self-esteem and character would begin to mature. The ranch was located at the end of what is now Via de San Ysidro with the main house facing Sycamore Street and within walking distance from the family home on West Park. Leadman (the ranch's namesake) was the name of the big beautiful black stallion in the front main corral. It was there the big horse would spend his time enjoying his retirement, mounting mares and making the kid's life miserable every time he entered his corral. At his old age he was still bold and mean-spirited; stomping around, back kicking and neighing, anything that could scare the kid out of his corral. But the kid had to teach this old boy that he was not going away. So, one time when the horse comes up from behind the kid and bites on the collar of his shirt, he swings around and smacks the horse with the back of the rake. The big animal backs off. Later the horse tries again and this time the kid taps him on the nose and the horse gets the point. To make friends the kid gives the horse the rake massage treatment and the old boy just loves it, never to bother him again.

The work was very tiring and what made it worse is that he couldn't hang out with the boys during the school year. But one of the main reasons he stayed on at the ranch was Katie, the rancher's daughter. About a week or so into working at the ranch he noticed a girl watching him from the window of her home. She looks to be about his age, 11 going on 12 or so. Soon she is hanging around the corrals he's working in and saying little things that annoy him.

"You left a little behind there; dad doesn't like to see stuff left behind."

She doesn't say "horseshit", but he does as he lowers a wheelbarrow full of it, turns around and tows the wheelbarrow to the spot she's pointing to and picks up the pieces of horseshit that are left. After a short while Katie is out there with him almost every day making small talk. He's shy, sweaty, sun-burnt and smells like horseshit, so he feels bad to get up close to her even though he would love to hold her hand. To him Katie is beautiful. Her long jet-black hair and big bright blue eyes reminds him of Elizabeth Taylor in the movie "National Velvet." And what's more, she could ride a horse! He never did see her mom and can't figure out where that beautiful head of black hair comes from, but she does have her dad's blue eyes. He begins to look forward to, working the ranch every day after school, never mind about hanging out with the boys. To him it feels like a secret love affair.

Then one day she walks over as she usually does.

"Last night at dinner dad said you are a very good worker, but that I should not be bothering you while you work."

If only Mr. Leadman knew it was because of Katie that you were such a "good worker." You want to tell dear old dad that you will soon marry his daughter and see what he says.

But of course, you don't actually say a thing like that. As the summer approaches Katie tells him she will be going away for the summer and after that will be enrolling in another school somewhere far away.

"I won't see you anymore?"

"I'm afraid so."

He knows now that come summer his "reason" for working this ranch will no longer be.

The summer arrives, Katie is gone and the kid no longer wants to work at the ranch. Hanging out with the boys is his only wish. One day he doesn't show up at the ranch and does not inform Mr. Leadman that he is quitting. Mr. Leadman finds Pop, complains that his kid did not even have the decency to tell him that he would be quitting and needs to find someone else to clean his corrals. Pop is mad and goes looking for the kid. He drives up in his pickup and gives you a scolding in front of the boys. He would never hit you, but you know he is really pissed-off. At dinner mom is also mad at you and asks why you quit.

"I just got tired of it."

Back then $5 dollars a day was a great help to the family with four kids to feed and Pop needed all the help he could get. He would show the kid what a great responsibility it was and how important he is to the family. The kid was very proud of himself when pop would talk that way to him, but he never forgot what he did at the Leadman Ranch. Later the kid goes back to working the ranches of San Ysidro. His favorite was Ocean Therapy Ranch right on the beach at the end of Monument Road. The area is now the Borderfield State Park (where the "imaginary line" once ran. Ironically, after all the violence, robberies, killings and rapes, they now call it Friendship Park.

At Ocean Therapy he loved to see how the handlers swam the big horses in the big round pool and the jock's riding them knee-deep on the beach. He wished he could do that, but his job was to clean corrals not ride horses. Later the ranch is shut down and the place is deserted. For a while during the mid-seventies it was the *"Gunslingers"* that tried to keep order in those hills from the drug smuggling, robberies, rapes and murders.

About a half-mile east of the Ocean Therapy ranch was The Ocean Rider Ranch. This ranch would, in just a few more years, play an important part in the life of the young man. Having worked at Ocean Rider for two summers he is well liked by the rancher and his family. A horse named "Big" also had an important role in his near future. When he is 19 years old, he comes back to the ranch and Ocean Rider becomes an important part of a plan he schemes up to smuggle weed across the nearby border.

Art Ayala, Ernie "Pipiolo" Leon, Danny Pacheco,
Julian Garcia at the Southwest Jr. High graduation.

5

SOUTHWEST JR. HIGH SCHOOL

The bus stop was behind the old library and all kids from Sidro were bused to the school about three miles from town. The school, established in 1929, was the same one Pop attended back in the '40s. At that time Pop's family lived right across the street, so close that on many occasions the school would announce on the loud speaker *"Joe, please come and get your chickens out of the school yard!"* He laughs when he tells you how the chickens would follow him to school.

At Southwest the boys are now more interested in girls. Before the start of the school year, a new kid had just moved into one of the two houses off the north end of Cottonwood Road, now the San Ysidro Health Center. Thor, the badass pitcher of your Tigers, lived in the other house. The new guy came from Otay he was different enough that the vatos weren't too sure how to treat this guy, but all were impressed by his style. Finely ironed khaki pants, sharp creases, a Pendleton shirt buttoned at the collar, shiny shoes and Elvis style pompadour hair slicked back with pomade—this new guy had a commanding presence, His name was Julian (RIP) and he was easily accepted into the Sidro vatos with no complaints. At the start of the school year they saw how easy it was for him to attract the girls. He always picked the prettiest white girl in the school and of course the girls were not from Sidro, but Imperial Beach or Palm City. At that time Southwest Jr. High School was the only junior high school in the area. Mar Vista Junior wouldn't open until much later.

Entering the seventh grade was exciting for the boy. His homeroom teacher was Mr. Parch, whom he grew to like very much and would be his homeroom teacher for the next three years. He remembers how every December 7th, Mr. Parch would tell the class about his experiences in World War II, he was in Hawaii aboard the USS Arizona, and he tells how lucky he was to be alive. He would get emotional telling the stories and the kids admired him for all he did to serve his country. He also remembers that day in ninth grade during his woodshop class when an announcement came over the loud speaker reporting that President John F. Kennedy had just been assassinated in Dallas, Texas. His woodshop teacher became very emotional and almost cried. He doesn't remember seeing any grown man from Sidro get emotional in that way and he doesn't think of his teachers as weak, but rather admired that they weren't afraid to show their feelings.

The vatos got good grades and began to become popular with the girls. At the start of the school year the vatos never even considered approaching the white girls, until they saw how easy it was for Julian! Since the girls were attracted to the Sidro vatos.

It becomes obvious to him that he also had no trouble getting girlfriends. One Saturday afternoon, he was visited by three girls from school, Connie, Nancy and Jane. They had walked a good three miles from Nestor and Palm City to his house on Bolton Hall Road. He didn't know what to do so he stayed inside the fence of his yard while the girls chatted with him from the outside of the fence. He doesn't know whether he should invite them in or what, then he turns and sees his mom giggling from their front window. He's very shy and has enough trouble talking with one girl, what is he supposed to do with three? Later that year Jane would become his "girlfriend", holding hands was about the only physical contact between the two. The relationship did not last long. Soon he would lose his virginity with a pretty white girl whom they called "Pudgy." By the seventh grade she was no longer pudgy.

> The night we met I knew I needed you so
> And if I had the chance, I'd never let you go
> So won't you say you love me
> I'll make you so proud of me

We'll make 'em turn their heads every place we go
So won't you, please, be my, be my baby[6]

Gwendolyn was her name, and he loved that name. Gwendolyn lives in the trailer park on Hollister Avenue across the street from the Purple Cow Dairy Mart, in Nestor Ca. On a Saturday afternoon she invites him over to her trailer, while her parents are away at work. He is nervous, but shows up anyhow. They sit and Gwendolyn is very eager to get intimate, they kiss and he is very moved by her big green eyes, as she gets more excited, her eyes become sexier to him. She unbuttons her blouse and guides his hands to her breasts. He had never seen or held such beautiful, big breasts like that. She guides him to her and they have sex. He thinks to himself "'I am now a man!"

Much later as an adult, he often remembers this first real sexual encounter of his life. But he has always wondered why he had been so timid, shy and very passive with women. He never really "went after a girl", never asserted himself, even when he was madly attracted to a certain girl. Even in the act of sex, it has always been the woman that makes the moves. Soon he discovers what might be the reason; the babysitter!

At the age of five years old, while they lived in Calexico, his parents had two sisters babysitting him and his siblings. The sisters, 14 and 17 years old, stayed at their home, a two-bedroom apartment. He and his 2 year old brother slept in one of the bedrooms, while his young sister of 3 years old slept with the parents. The youngest babysitter slept with the brothers, it appears that his mother and father did not think anything of it, and there was nowhere else the girls could sleep, the older sister already was sleeping on the only couch in the house.

Little brother Tury, slept at the foot of the bed, while he and babysitter Rita would sleep side-by-side. On that first night Rita begins to caress his body, eventually going down to his underpants. She caressing his penis becomes a nightly ritual. At first he is confused about what is going on, his penis

---

[6] *Be My Baby*, The Ronettes, August 1963

does get hard and she allows him to caress her breasts, soon he wants to explore her lower parts, but she does not let him.

These nightly sex games continued for several months, the young boy would eagerly run to bed at bedtime, until that one afternoon that his mom comes home early from work and finds his father in bed with the older sister, the boy was at school at the time in Kindergarten. Like always he would run home to see Rita, this time she is not home. The mom informs him that the girls will no longer live at the home. Sometime later he finds out what really happened and he never tells his mom about Rita.

The school administration, at Southwest Jr. High, considered the vatos troublesome with the way they dressed and strutted around school with the vice-principal constantly hovering over them, looking to catch them in whatever no-good activities they might be up to. He'd even show up at the bus stop in the mornings to catch the vatos smoking cigarettes, so he could suspend them from school. The vice-principal would demand the boys to raise their hands, so he could smell for any tobacco on their fingers. Someone got the wise idea one morning to smear the seeds from the pepper leaves of nearby trees, onto their fingers, which produced a pungent odor. That day, when the vice-principal smelled their fingers he flinched back violently from the awful smell. This only made him madder and they were suspended anyway. Giving out suspensions and "swats" were his choice of punishment. One time you were suspended from school just for speaking Spanish in the school hallways.

The house on Bolton Hall Rd was picked out by Pop because it was less than 50 yards from Bob White's horse hauling business. He had a huge garage at the end of Bolton Hall Rd next to the river bottom. In this garage were his three big rigs and trailers for hauling horses from the race track to parts unknown to him. As soon as Pop sees the house for rent he doesn't hesitate to rent it and moves his family there. It was perfect. After long hauls and at all hours of the day or night, he would simply park the rig, lock everything up and walk the few steps back to his house and rest.

At 13 years old the boy is starting to become a man. And It is at this house that he begins to realize a new sense of maturity building inside of him.

Their neighbors are the Guevara family, Bobby the eldest of twelve kids lived next door with their mom, he learns to love Mama Francis and her family, and she's recently widowed and has a big job raising such a big family. Every day she fixes a big stack of flour tortillas, rice and beans, and he loves it when he is invited over for dinner. They all sit around a big park bench to eat.

Bobby is 16 years old, obese, like all his siblings. Bobby has a 1954 blue Ford station wagon. It seems to him that Bobby doesn't have very many friends, maybe because of his weight. In the afternoons they sit in his car drinking bubble-up and smoking Newport cigarettes. Bobby loves music and they spend the afternoon listening to what are now called *"the oldies."* Bobby teaches him about music; *James Brown, The Temptations, The Rolling Stones,* and others.

> *"Now listen to this song. Hear the lead guitar? Catch the bass playing, now the drums."*

He talks as he bops his head up and down and does the *"air guitar,"* tapping on his steering wheel for the drums. This was the beginning of his great love affair with music. Soon he introduces Bobby to the vatos de Sidro. He is quickly accepted and becomes a vato de Sidro. He's the eldest of the group and all the vatos come to love him. Soon they tag him with his Sidro name *"The Bun."*

One day he, George and Guero were using BB guns to shoot birds off a tree and when they fell to the ground, we'd grab them. Guero, who also lived on Bolton Hall Rd., was always on the lookout for birds, some big enough to eat. One time at the hills he grabbed a live pheasant that had been hiding in a bush because it had a broken wing. We started walking to his house and Guero starts plucking the live bird under his arm. There was a trail of feathers all the way down to Bolton Hall Rd. At his house he kills the bird, cuts it up and finds the bird has eggs inside with yolks that had not yet hardened into shells. Guero turns the open breast over the heated pan and cooked and ate the fried eggs. He and George were grossed out.

On the dove hunt that day they approached a large oak and spotted what appeared to be a body hanging off a rope on one of the limbs. They halt, and someone screams and Guero says

> "Wait, it looks like it's only a dummy. Someone is trying to scare us off, let's get closer."

As they near, they can see that it really is a body hanging there. Guero goes up to it and sees that the man is wearing a big ring. He tries to take it off and they see that part of the skin on the finger is beginning to separate. The stench finally reaches them, and they scream. They run off scared to death. They run to his house to tell his mom and as they enter the kitchen, they see a cooked beef head on the table. It was the same color as the hanging man and the eyes were all bugged. His uncle was visiting from Mexicali and they decided to cook a beef head that day. All three of them were now very frightened and they tell his mom what they had just discovered. His mom calls the police. The three boys are interviewed, which re-traumatizes them. The detective says they must take him to the scene to recreate how they found the body. They retrace their steps and as they approach the body the police are about to cut it down from the tree. When they do the body falls to the ground making a god-awful noise; its bones cracking and rotted flesh flopping. The stench was unbearable. The detective could see that the boys had seen enough and led them away from the scene. He's sure that his friends had nightmares the way he did for months after.

George suggested they call radio station KCBQ for the $24 it was paying out related to news regarding the incident. They did and divided up the money, trying their best to forget the whole experience for now. But couldn't. Everyone in the barrio wanted to know the whole story so they were forced to relive it over and over again.

Upon coming home from school one afternoon, the boy stumbles upon his parents having a loud argument in the kitchen. Pop sees him come in and gives him a look he hadn't seen before—a look of hurt. Pop left the house but came back later that evening.

The next day Pop is at the school bus drop-off.

"Get in, I want you to see something," he tells him. They drive up to Hall Avenue, he takes a right into the alley, U-turns and stops at the corner just up from the old Mt. Carmel church. He keeps looking over to the church, looks at his watch and then they see a car backing out of the driveway of the church residence. The car goes past them and Pop follows, down to the boulevard and heads east. He enters the parking lot of the Toreador Motel.

"Look who is getting off."

"It's the Priest!"

As the priest heads towards one of the rooms a woman appears slowly walking in his direction and they both enter the room.

"What are they doing?"

"What the hell do you think they're doing? They are not going in that room to pray! She will get down on her knees alright, but not to pray!"

"You mean they are going to fuck?"

"You goddamned right! That's the reason your mom and I had that big argument yesterday. I know that motherfucker has been going over to our house to "visit and pray" so your mother says. Did you see what he wasn't wearing?"

"Yeah, he wasn't wearing his robes and that white thing they wear around their neck."

"Yeah "the collar" they call it. I don't ever want to see that motherfucker in my house again. I hope you can tell your mother what you just saw."

He does tell his mother what he saw, and that priest never came back to the house. Those were powerful adult reality lessons that he learned at only 13 years old.

That first year at Southwest J. High, a friendship and strong bond matured with Julian and the vatos who made him the unofficial leader of the small group from Sidro. Julian would later become your compadre after you baptize his and Doris' first daughter.

One incident that secured Julian's spot as unofficial leader came because of a quarrel over a girl. This Latina beauty lived in Old Town National City and liked Julian when he lived in Otay. One of the OTNC vatos liked this girl too but she kept bringing up Julian. This vato wanted to show her who is the baddest and sends word to Sidro that he wants a showdown with Julian. Phone booth numbers are exchanged, the call is made and words are thrown.

> *"I have my vatos, you bring your vatos and we'll see who is the baddest!"*

The spot that was selected was right off of the railroad tracks in front of the old Big Sky drive-in, down from Main Street on Industrial Blvd.

> *"Let's go kick some OTNC ass!"*

There were six vatos. Julian, Danny, Art, Cesar, Turco and him. Armed with bike chains and bats the Sidro vatos walk the railroad tracks just past Palm City to the agreed upon location.

The vatos are walking on the tracks when they spot the OTNC vatos coming close to the Main Street overpass. They halt on each side of the bridge. Julian goes forward.

> *"Orale puto's, let's throw chingazos! (OK you faggots, let's get it on!)*

As he yells out the Sidro vatos pan out behind Julian and the OTNC vatos see the bats and chains. They are outnumbered and poorly armed, so they turn and run back north in all directions.

> *"Pinches puto's culeros!" (Fucking pussies!)*

The Sidro vatos are pumped up with pride, yelling and whooping and thumping their chests when suddenly someone yells out:

> *"Trucha La Jura! "(the cops!),*

Bats and chains are flung to the other side of the tracks as they spot the patrol car slowly coming toward them below on Industrial Blvd. As the patrol car comes to a stop right below them the door opens and they see a familiar smile.

> *"El Jura de Sidro!" Sgt. Kelly, the Sidro cop!*
> *"Get your asses down from there!"*

The vatos climb down the railroad embankment towards the police officer.

> *"I saw you throw your bats and chains down the other side. What about those boys running down the tracks? They weren't running away because of me, they didn't even have time to see me before they started running off like scared jack rabbits! I wonder what could have scared them off like that."*

The vatos just kind of shrug.

"Ok, let's take you back to Sidro," he says. (Without rolling the 'r' he pronounces it like Seed-dro) The vatos look at each other and roll their eyes back, giggling.

> *"So how did you know we were here?"* Julian asked

> *"Hell, I've been following ya'll since you left Seed-dro. I was very curious as to what you were fixin' to do with those sticks, bats and chains, walking on the railroad tracks. Come on, you know damn well that this will not end well. Those boys don't take too kindly to being scared off in that way, you know they will try something to save face so watch your backs."*

All six crowd into the patrol car victorious and happy to be taken back to Sidro. They ask Sgt. Kelly if they could turn on the siren as they go into Sidro. He obliges. With sirens blaring he drops the vatos off at the park behind the Civic Center. It must have been quite a sight for anyone in the park that afternoon—six 15 and 16-year-old badass vatos piling out of a patrol car laughing and giggling like silly little boys.

Sgt. Kelly was well liked with the Sidro vatos because he never talked down to them and stopped to talk with them on the street whenever he could asking in a joking way, *"what no-good are ya'll up to now?"* Sgt. Kelly would later join the BARF squad of gunslingers, killing and shooting border bandits in no-man's land only to have his personal life upended in the end with some trauma disorder, the likes of which most of the BARF'ers got.

The OTNC vatos do return for revenge one night shortly after the incident. The guys at the library spot two cars that are not from the barrio that make the left turn up West Park looking for their payback. The vatos at the library sound the alarm by whistling to the vatos at the park. They move quickly. As they reach the tennis courts out runs Catchie, the fastest vato in the barrio. With a big rock in his hand he runs up to the lead car and before they even see him he hurls it at the windshield, smashing it and takes off. They didn't know what hit them and soon after Sgt. Kelly and his backup were chasing them in their patrol cars. They're stopped at the park and arrested for carrying weapons. Sgt. Kelly later tells the vatos they'd confiscated two 38-caliber revolvers.

By the time he's 16 he had saved the $100 he needed to buy the car he wanted. Guero's father was selling his old 1954 red and white four-door Chevy. It was rusted in places, but it was his grand prize and ticket to freedom.

6

MAR VISTA HIGH SCHOOL

D espite earning A's and B's throughout junior and high school, by his senior year in 1967, he begins losing his motivation to complete his education. The teen, once very interested in academics, begins to feel unmotivated and the disillusionment begins. All of a sudden, everything about school begins to feel irrelevant and he began "ditching school". He felt disconnected from everything around him, but he doesn't know exactly why. Was it the fact that the family was always moving from house to house? In San Ysidro alone, they had lived in eight different houses. The changes had him in five different elementary schools, including Beyer, Balboa, Encanto, Horton and then back to San Ysidro at Sunset Elementary, where he graduates the sixth grade. He was tired of always being The FNG (Fucking New Guy), getting into fights at each new school and trying hard just to fit in.

The last move was to his rival barrio Otay, south of Chula Vista. In those days what separated the two barrios was the great Otay Mesa; free of the sprawling housing tracts that now fill it, and the beautiful Otay River Valley.

Living in the middle of his rival barrio, he does not want to be seen in the streets, but he does have to enroll into another school, Castle Park High School. He hated everyday he was there and away from his friends. His '54 Chevy has motor problems and is not running. He works hard at getting it fixed, and when the old car is up and running, he asks his mom if he could enroll back at Mar Vista High.

Now back at Mar Vista High School in Imperial Beach, he drives to school every morning from Otay. It feels good to be back with his boys from Sidro. He is still very shy when it comes to girls, but has no problem attracting them. In fact, one girl who his best friend nicknamed "Little Egypt" (after a current rock song), would be the first to break his teenage heart. They were in dreamy puppy love, out on Friday's nights at the drive-in in his 54 Chevy, making out in the back seat.

> 'Cast my memory back there, Lord
> Sometimes I'm overcome thinking about
> Making love in the green grass
> Behind the stadium
> With you, my brown-eyed girl
> You my brown-eyed girl'[7]

But their little love boat was short-lived. Little Egypt's mom didn't approve of her going out with some guy from San Ysidro, so she was sent away to Texas. She sends letters and pictures and you miss her, but life must go on. He meets other girls and Little Egypt would later end up marrying another Sidro vato.

As he enters his senior year the family moves again, this time back to San Ysidro and into the house on Cottonwood Road. The '54 Chevy breaks down for good and needs to be junked so his uncle gives him a '59 blue Mercury, the model with the push-button gear shift—but "hey it's a car"!

It's at this time something begins to alter within him. School no longer gives him the same feelings it once did. He begins to feel alienated and bored and starts looking for a change. Ditching becomes a regular thing and he's able to convince some of his friends to go along with him. He would drive up to the bus stop where the boys were waiting and wave at them to come with him to Tijuana, or better yet Rosarito and Ensenada.

---

[7] "Bown-Eyed Girl" Van Morrison, March 1967

Because of repeated truancies the school counselor ultimately called him into her office telling him he will never go to college and should consider taking metal or woodshop classes in order to save himself. He begins to feel like an outcast and becomes rebellious and angry.

One day before high school graduation Pop takes him aside and tells him that he can no longer support him.

> *"There are too many mouths to feed in this house," he tells him. "You should take that girl you are seeing, marry her and find your own place."*

He stopped attending school all together and began to prepare for the coming changes. Marriage had to happen, so it was arranged that he would wed the girl he is seeing on September 2, 1967.

7

SMUGGLER'S GULCH

Smugglers Gulch Today

At an early age most; kids in San Ysidro were exposed to marijuana by older guys in the neighborhood. They admired these older vatos and daily saw them smoking weed. They could see how easy it was to get weed in Tijuana and they crossed regularly at the behest of their moms to buy tortillas and other items. In 1968 there were no drug sniffing dogs at the border and they soon learned early how easy it was to get a newspaper roll of marijuana across. Most importantly, they learned there was money to be made in doing this.

Financially, married life was hard. The couple was constantly looking for apartments because they were unable to come up with the rent. To make ends meet he started selling small amounts of weed. First were baggies known as lids, then a kilo here and a kilo there. Most of his customers were from Imperial Beach, Chula Vista and National City. The Polleros, the guys who lead the pollos for money, would also buy a few kilos to take to Los Angeles.

Business was brisk, and paranoia wasn't as palatable as it would later become. During this time there wasn't a need to be armed so violence was seldom seen. We all knew who was doing what, most of the time working together on special loads. Transactions were made over laughter, beers and joints. No one thought of themselves as gangsters and there were no "crews" yet.

It was too easy to get kilos of weed across that "Imaginary line." One special place he used once was called Smuggler's Gulch—the same place that Joseph Wambaugh describes in *Lines and Shadows* where shootings, murder, robberies and rape would occur on a nightly basis. Smugglers Gulch is about a half-mile from The Ocean Rider Ranch and the perfect place to catch duffel bags full of weed. The Imaginary Line at the top had only four strands of barbed wire that separated the U.S. from Mexico, right next to the road that leads to Las Playas beach in Tijuana. The plan sounded simple enough; just have your contacts in Tijuana drive up to the place, park and throw the duffel bags down the gulch and you've got your merchandise. But as he envisions the plan he realizes it would be hard for a couple of skinny guys lugging four full duffel bags each of weed down the hill, through shrubs, cactus and rattlesnakes. He asks Cesar and Turco to help. Their eyes lit up at the offer.

Cesar had not yet been drafted into the Army. When he is, he gets shipped off to Vietnam where he does two tours and returns with a very bad case Post-Traumatic Stress Disorder. He will not be allowed to leave El Paso, Texas, where he is under house arrest for committing some kind of terrorist act. His PTSD has cost him dearly as far as being able to communicate with his wife and daughter. They can't figure out what Cesar is trying to say most of the time and eventually stop taking his calls.

A few years later, Turco will be murdered in Tijuana. He's not sure how.

Each duffel bag could carry anywhere from eight to 10 kilos of weed, totaling more than 25 pounds. Sounds too risky. So, he thinks about how to get the weed to the car waiting on Monument Road and his big idea hits him like a pile of bricks.

> *"We could use horses! We would need to bring along a couple of good wire brushes to wipe off the prickly and very sharp cactus spines to protect the horses. They would have to just lug up the duffel bags to the saddle horns—two to each horse, and then we ride down to the car, load up the weed and that's it!"*

It's time to go visit the rancher down the road and ask him to rent them the horses for a ride to the beach. The driver of the car will hide among the trees at the bottom of the gulch.

The plan is set. They drive down to the ranch and he asks about the old owner of the rancher.

> *"Naw, he passed on some years ago." "Oh, sorry to hear that. He was a good man and a good boss too."*

He tells the new rancher how as a kid he had worked this ranch and asks about "Big."

> *"Yeah, that ol' horse is still here—still strong, mean and feisty."*

> *"Could we rent ol' Big and another horse for a ride down the beach this weekend?"*

> *"I reckon so, just for a few hours?"*

> *"Yeah just to the beach and back for old times' sake."*

> *"May I go see ol' Big?*

"Yeah he's still in the same corral, over there."

"Oh, one more thing. May I come by a couple of times next week? Just so Big and I can get comfortable again? Maybe he still remembers me. I'd like to walk him around the track, just reins. I'll bareback him, OK?"

"Yeah sure, just groom and feed him afterwards."

He goes up to Big's corral. The big horse comes up to greet him. He looks the same. He rubs his huge forehead.

"Remember me when you and I were just youngsters?" He thinks back to the time he worked this ranch and about all the experiences he's gone through. *"So much has happened since I last saw you big boy!"*

He calls his connection in Tijuana to set the plan for the weed delivery. It must happen at the time we agreed upon. We don't want to be standing around on two horses, looking out of place doing nothing when the Border Patrol makes passes in the area. It will be the responsibility of the third man to be the lookout for the green jeeps, and when they are far enough away he will send the signal to the two on horseback to quickly pick up the bags.

On Monday morning he goes to the ranch, brushes off Big, puts the bridle bit into Big's mouth and walks him out to the track. He jumps up on the horse bareback and begins walking him around. The front part of the track is next to Monument Road and atop of Big he has a clear view of the ridgeline, east and west of Smuggler's Gulch. He is looking for the green Border Patrol jeep. Suddenly he spots a jeep just east of the gulch. He checks his watch: 9:37 a.m. As the jeep heads east, he sees something that he had not thought of. The Border Patrol officer gets out of the jeep and with binoculars scans the whole area.

"This is going to take more planning. Our lookout will need binoculars and the riders will need legging chaps like the ones the cowboys wear. The pickup and loading of the weed will have to be quicker than I thought. We can't be stopping to pick off cactus spines

from our legs. After the Tijuana guys throw the bags over the fence, wearing chaps and circling around the horses at the bottom of the gulch will look more natural to the Border Patrol. We will look like regular ranch guys, exercising our horses."

Checking his watch, he keeps circling Big. It's been more than an hour and no other patrol jeeps have been by the area.

The plan is set. He will take Cesar, the better rider with him and Turco will be the look-out. Turco has a loud, mouth whistle.

"The whole operation must not take more than two hours. If it does, we are busted! For less than two hours of work I am willing to pay each of you $500 dollars and I can only pay you after I make the $6,000 to pay for the weed, wadda ya say?"

He calls his contact in Tj, instructs him on how the operation must take place since he will not have any further contact with the TJ guys. He will have four strong men to fling the bags far enough into the gulch one at a time so as to not show much activity. They must be there at exactly 10 a.m. Each canvas bag will carry 10 kilos. Turco will use binoculars as the look-out. Two whistles mean the coast is clear, one whistle – stop! Border Patrol in sight.

On the day of the operation things go just as planned. The bags landed far enough into the gulch and were easy to retrieve. They heaved the bags onto the saddle horns, one on each side of the horse and trotted back to the car where Turco is waiting to load up the trunk. When they're done the two head back to the ranch. In less than two hours they had pulled off the operation. Time to celebrate!

The going rate at the time for a kilo of weed was between, $450 to $500. His supplier's price for him in Tijuana was $150 per kilo, plus another $200 for the guys flinging the bags over the fence. At $500 each he stands to make $20,000, minus expenses from the 40 kilos. The plan worked out better than he could have imagined, but he only did it that one time. It was too risky and too much work. Besides, cars stashed with weed in the trunks, tires and anywhere else were already coming across the border.

Despite the large amount of money, he'd just earned, it went quickly. He was always irresponsible with cash and foolishly spent it, usually in amounts he never had. In the culture of poverty, saving and handling money wisely is not often a priority since they never had an opportunity to do so.

"The Ocean Rider Operation," as he comes to call it, earns him a reputation with the drug dealers in Tijuana and gets him acquainted with some up and coming big time dealers—the ones that survived the wild shoot outs and drug wars for the rights of the now famous "Tijuana-San Ysidro Plaza." These are the guys who would form what is now called *"The Tijuana Cartel."*

But soon the drug dealing life would be interrupted by a wave of protests for social injustice against Mexican-American barrios across the Southwest.

8

"LA CAUSA"
(THE CHICANO MOVEMENT)

The Brown Berets at Chicano Park,
photo courtesy of Geronimo Blanco

In 1968 Mexican-American students were walking out of the classrooms of Mar Vista High, joining in solidarity with students in Los Angeles, San Francisco in protest of an anti-discrimination movement at the hands of teachers and "the system."

It's during this time he's approached by some of these younger activists who tell him that some guys from San Diego State University were looking to unite the barrio with something called the "Chicano Movement" or "La Causa!" What the university students were looking for was someone from the barrio that could reach out to the vatos in Sidro and form a chapter of the Brown Berets. The following is an excerpt from Wikipedia describing the Brown Berets:

The Brown Berets (Los Boinas Cafes) is a pro-Chicano organization founded by David Sanchez in the late 60s during the Chicano Movement and remains active today. The Brown Beret movements largely revolved around farm worker's struggles, educational reform, and anti-war activism. They have also organized against police brutality, with many groups staying active since the passage of California Proposition 187.

In 1966, as part of the Annual Chicano Student Conference in Los Angeles County, a team of high school students discussed issues affecting Mexican Americans in their barrios and schools. Among the students at the conference were Vickie Castro, Jorge Licón, David Sanchez, Rachel Ochoa, and Moctesuma Esparza.[3] These high school students formed the Young Citizens for Community Action the same year and worked together to support Dr. Julian Nava's campaign as a Los Angeles school board member candidate in 1967.[3] Sanchez and Esparza had trained with Father John B. Luce's Social Action Training center at the Church of the Epiphany (Episcopal) in Lincoln Heights and with the Community Service Organization.[4]

The organization's name was then changed to Young Chicanos For Community Action or "YCCA".[5] In 1967, the YCCA founded the Piranya Coffee House. In September 1967, Sal Castro, a Korean War veteran and teacher at Lincoln High School, met YCCA members at the coffee house. The group decided to wear brown berets as a symbol of unity and resistance against discrimination. As a result, the organization gained the name "Brown Berets." Their agenda was to fight police harassment, inadequate public schools, health care and job opportunities, minority education issues, a lack of political representation, and the Vietnam War. It set up branches in Texas, New Mexico, Colorado, New York, Florida, Chicago,

St. Louis and other metropolitan areas with large "raza" populations. The ideology of the Brown Berets was primarily represented by **Chicanismo**.

He was up for the task of recruiting and organizing the young people of San Ysidro, his Barrio. And thus began education in earnest on the politics of the Chicano Movement. Around this timeframe he is also approached by the then director of the MAAC Project (Mexican American Advisory Council) to open and direct the first San Ysidro Teen Post. It would be located at the church hall of the old Mount Carmel Church on Hall Avenue. The position came with a salary that was desperately needed since he wasn't doing much dealing during that period. Also, the idea of having a center to use for the barrio vatos was intriguing. Get the kids off the streets and educate them in the politics of the Chicano Movement. He accepted both propositions.

The "Movement" became his passion and as his ideology expanded his self-esteem grew and leadership skills began to unfold. He began to feel like a whole new person and dives into the movement literature.

Books like *Eldridge Cleaver's Soul on Ice*, *Che Guevara's Diary* and Chairman Mao's *Little Red Book* were the first of his required reading. The movement not only expanded his networks and contacts for the Brown Berets but also his customer base for weed. In 1969 most if not all college students in the movement were smoking weed. It quickly became a hot commodity and while he prospered some, he had to back off the business because of the events that followed.

Soon after opening the Teen Post he received a visit from an FBI agent who informs him that in the Mission District of San Francisco seven Brown Berets had been involved in the shooting and killing of a policeman. He says that while six of them were arrested one of them is on the run and heading south. The FBI believed he was headed for Mexico and would make a stop in San Ysidro to contact the local Brown Berets for cover and help getting across the border.

He did not know it yet, but this incident that occurred more than 900 miles to the north on his 20th birthday would affect him profoundly in the very near future.

The shooting as reported in many media outlets at the time, Ramparts Magazine:

Los Siete de la Raza

Los Siete de la Raza was the label given to seven Mission District San Francisco California young men, approached by two plainclothes policemen while alleged to have been moving a stereo or TV into a house at 429-433 Alvarado Street on May 1, 1969 at around 10:30 a.m. The altercation left one officer, Joe Brodnik, dead from a gunshot wound from the other officer's weapon. When police descended on the crime scene, they entered the house and fired automatic rifles into the second story ceiling in the assumption the suspects were hiding in the attic after which they flooded the building with tear gas as a helicopter hovered overhead; they sent a fire truck ladder up to the roof to facilitate the search while officer Brodnik's corpse lay untended on the sidewalk (local press reports).

In Santa Cruz, seven youths were arrested for the murder of SFPD undercover officer Brodnik and attempted murder of partner Paul McGoran, as well as burglary. They were defended by activist lawyers Charles Garry and Richard Hodge and written up by the Left press, including Ramparts Magazine. The young Latinos included four Salvadorans, one Nicaraguan, and one Honduran, some of whom had been involved in the youth group, the Mission Rebels (founded in 1965), and later in pan-Latino organizations such as COBRA (Confederation of Brown Race for Action) at the College of San Mateo, and the Brown Berets.

When confronted by FBI agents, he tells them the truth, that he does not know who these Berets were and knows nothing about the shooting up north (information took longer to reach everyone then). The FBI agent tells him they have set up a surveillance operation for the wanted man in San Ysidro; the man's name is George Lopez.

He soon notices that he is being followed as he drives to work in the morning and back. He also suspects that the phones at the teen center and at home are being tapped into. At that time, he and his wife were living at his mother-in-law's house and one day while his younger brother-in-law was at the house, three FBI agents came to the door and scared the boy into letting them into the house. They searched the whole house but only came away with my selected reading material.

Despite the FBI's presence and no word of the capture of George Lopez, the Teen Post became a hub of activity for the young Chicanos participating in "La Causa." They were seen proudly walking the streets of San Ysidro wearing their new Brown Berets while they were getting stopped and harassed by local police. The first Cadre of Berets of San Ysidro was made up by his "lieutenant" Geronimo Blanco, (currently the National Commander of the Brown Berets), his brother Tury, brother-in-law Ruben, Francisco, and Remejio. Together they would recruit the teenagers of Sidro.

At first Brown Beret activity consisted of providing back up security for Movement leaders who came into town to speak at college events. Those included visionaries such as Cesar Chavez, Rodolfo "Corky" Gonzalez, and Reyes Tijerina. When they came into town it was always the San Ysidro chapter of the berets who were the first to be called in and it was an honor for them to perform this sacred duty. Brown Beret security included 10 to 15 members dressed in full regalia ready at a moment's notice to provide backup for leaders who were always in danger of attacks from right-wing extremists.

One night while Mr. Tijerina was speaking at the University of California, San Diego, we received a report that his house was bombed with Molotov cocktails. Fortunately, no one was home at the time, but the incident still called for additional security. That night he volunteered to guard Mr. Tijerina in his motel room. As his security he sat up all night in that room with a .357 Magnum strapped to his waist, while Mr. Tijerina slept.

In early 1969 Rodolfo *"Corky"* Gonzalez called for a three-day Chicano Unity Conference to be held in Denver, at the headquarters for his "La Crusada" movement. He was asked to attend and the assistant director,

Mrs. Solis would watch the teen post during his trip. And just like that he packed up a little VW bug and headed to Denver. It would prove to be the most exhilarating event he'd ever attended. Chicanos Movement leaders from other states attended the conference in a show of solidarity leaving him with an immense feeling of inspiration.

But that excitement would not last, because upon returning from Denver he learned that for some unexplained reason the teen post had been shut down. He and Mrs. Solis suspected the FBI convinced MAAC to shut the center due to Brown Beret activity.

Amazingly things took a turn for the better, about three months after the center was shut down, when a local professor who everybody called Tio Eddy, nominated him to receive a fellowship from California State University, Sacramento. Eddy was heavily involved in founding this program, in which 20 students were selected statewide to study and become bilingual educators, all expenses paid. Painfully aware of his dire situation he jumped at the opportunity to get out of San Ysidro and headed north to begin a whole new life. His decision upset some members of the Berets and soon rumors began to circulate that he had sold out the movement—somehow collaborated with the FBI and skipped town out of fear. But later the reasons for his abrupt exit became clear to all.

His movement brother and second in command Geronimo Blanco, took over the local Beret operation and ultimately became the National Commander of the Brown Berets. He still is to this day.

9

LIFE AS A COLLEGE STUDENT IN SACRAMENTO

The Mexican-American Undergraduate Fellowship for Bilingual Education was funded by the administration of then California Governor Edmund Brown, father of current Governor Jerry Brown. Upon arrival at Sacramento State in September of 1969, he was assigned a room at the Westridge student dorms and quickly got to work going through orientation activities. Administrators treated the new students as if they were sons and daughters, making sure they knew how much work was put into bringing the program to life. The new students were called "Felitos" (an endearing term that referred to them as "undergrads"). The program would be the example for future programs on a national level. Everything was riding on their shoulders for the future generations of young Chicanos. The commitment that his fellow students showed motivated him to keep going. In his first two years he had earned the Dean's Honor List back to back and bought a car through the student loan program—a cream colored, 1970 WV square back Volkswagen.

At Sac State he had the yet unknown privilege to study under the now renowned Chicano artists and Movement leaders of the time; Esteban Villa and Jose Montoya. Together they formed the "Royal Chicano Air Force" and would travel California's barrios to promote Chicano art and culture. In San Diego their work is part of the beautiful murals of Chicano Park.

In Jose's class on Chicano Culture and Art, he inspired the class to put on a play of the current book the class had been studying; Octavio Paz's "Mosaico Mexicano." For dress rehearsal the Felitos wore robes of black and white and their faces were painted as such. He asks the young man from San Diego:

"So, what are you going to do in the play since you do not want to be on stage?" "I don't know," he replies.

"You can be the Director!"

"I don't know how to be a director of a play, what if I play the guitar?"

Jose laughs out loud and says, *"Good, you can be the guitar-playing director!"*

The whole class laughs with him. Jose had a laugh that could light up a room. The whole class grew to love and admire both of them. Rehearsals became the highlight of the school day. The guitar-playing director would strum while the cast would go through movements of the play.

Soon the cast was ready to go on the road. The first show would be at Sacramento City College, then on to Stanford. At Stanford he would get noticed and was later offered a scholarship into a Post graduate program. The theater group played at Davis University where the show was a hit with local Chicano students at each of the colleges. After the show, cast member Ruben, took a painting from one of the halls and gave it to the guitar-playing director. Ruben was a real left-wing rebel. He stated that he never stole from the "system" but rather just "liberates stuff." One summer Ruben joins "las Brigadas," students who signed up to pick sugar cane in Cuba and get an education Cuban Revolution style. That painting by Diego Rivera titled "The Flower Vendor" still hangs on the guitar-playing director's wall.

Everything was going well. Getting A's was routine for him, but he soon begins to tire of living in the dorms. He had not yet started selling drugs, mainly because he did not have the connections and market. But from the stipend he received he could rent a small one-bedroom house and bring his wife up to Sacramento. In that same year after coming to stay with him she no longer wants to live there and asked him if she could move back to San Diego to be with her mom. He wasn't going to force to stay and agreed. During the second year his son was born on June 11, 1970. He is named Ariel.

The Anthropology department at Sacramento State had planned a month-long study tour of middle and Southern Mexico for the class to get a heavy dose of Mexican and indigenous culture. The study tour would be led by non-other than Tio Eddy and Professor Diego. There was one catch. His son was due to be born two days after the class left for Mexico so he stayed behind in San Diego to be there for when his son was born. The following day he gets on a plane to Mexico City to catch up with his classmates who by now would be in Oaxaca. He gets off the plane and takes the 12-hour bus ride to the capital. Arriving in the morning he finally catches up with his classmates who are staying at the Marques del Valle hotel downtown, across the street from the Zocalo (the center plaza of every Mexican city).

They were on their way to San Cristobal de Las Casas, Chiapas! That whole month they visited many cities, archeological and historic sites meeting with Mexican students to exchange dialogue and ideas. The group also traveled through the states of Michoacán, Guanajuato, Queretaro, and the state of Mexico. In Paracho, Michoacán, where one can buy the finest guitars in all of Mexico, he buys a beautiful six-string guitar and met the Maestro and his family in the very place the guitar was made. In just a few short years that guitar would be used for purposes other than music.

They stayed four days in Oaxaca, taking in the sights. Little did he know that living in this magnificent city at the same time was a skinny 11-year-old girl who would become his future third wife? She told him later they very likely crossed paths as she and her friends would often hang out at the zocalo to watch and giggle at the hippies who came to visit as tourists, very likely for the Dona Rosa's magic mushrooms that were famous all over the world. He was surely one of the hippie-looking guys that walked by that day, since they did stay a Sunday in Oaxaca during the same summer she had lived there.

Back in Sacramento, his wife is still insisting to stay with her mom; he begins to immerse himself into the student life style. Hippies, drugs, sex and rock 'n' roll was the popular trend. He lets his hair grow and begins to meet many new friends who were constantly getting high on weed and cocaine, he also starts playing and jamming on his guitar with them. He had also found a new market. On his trips back home he began to bring small amounts of weed and cocaine.

The demand grew. Now he was practically living at airports. He had a locker at LAX that he used as his personal closet but at some point, things took a turn for the worst and he would end up having to leave in that locker a fine hand-stitched leather suitcase he had purchased in Leon, Guanajuato. The suitcase wasn't expensive but did have sentimental value, having traveled with him during some very dangerous trips.

"There he goes" as Eric Burdon of the Animals would sing, *"a skinny long-haired leaping gnome,"* wearing boots holding two ounces of cocaine and a guitar case with two more ounces in it. At that time there were no drug-sniffing dogs at the airports and truth be told he just looked too outrageous for anyone to suspect that he was dealing cocaine. There were huge profits to be made from just six ounces of coke. It was the new thing in town and everyone wanted a nose-full.

10

SEX, DRUGS AND ROCK 'N' ROLL

One of his fellow "Felitos" classmates was singing in a rock band that needed help getting gigs. The band called themselves the *"East-West Band"*, as the drug-money gets better, he suggests to his friend, Freddy, they look for a big house to rent and move in with the band. They found a four-bedroom house on Folsom Blvd. that was perfect. It had a large living room for band practice and plenty of space for instruments, amps and equipment. He told the band members that he would act as the manager of the band and find the gigs. The band had been playing occasionally at a night club called "La Cabana" outside the city limits near the Sacramento River. He decided to tell its owner that the band is sounding much better and assured him they could fill the club with customers during the week because of its large following. The fanfare mostly came from cocaine and weed customers, but they would surely come to hear the band. Sal, the owner agreed to give them a try at three nights a week.

The East-West Band was made up of Vietnam vet Freddy who was the lead singer, his brother Roger on drums, Kenny, the only white boy of the group—a Chicago bluesman on lead guitar, Harold on bass and Timmy (who was blind) on the keyboards. They were all talented in their own right.

They later added back-up singers Irma and Patricia. Irma was also in their Felitos program. They would be dubbed, "The Chi-Chi Sisters" and when they did Malo's *"Suavecito"* the house came down.

The band was a hit and they filled the club each night they played covering great songs of the time from Santana, Malo, Tower of Power, Chicago, the Stones and many more. People came to listen, dance and get high on cocaine, the latter for which he had found the perfect front. As the manager he sat in the audience dealing, networking and meeting women he'd end up having love affairs with. But eventually a consequence caught up with the lover boy and he feels pain in his penis and sees blood in his urine, so he goes to the school clinic.

"Yeah babe you got it!" the nurse tells him.

"Got what?"

"The Clap! Gonorrhea! You're going to have to give me the name of the girl."

"But I don't know who it is."

"What do you mean; you don't know who it is? You got that many girls that you don't know which one infected you? Here, pull your pants down and turn around." The nurse jabs him with the syringe.

"In three days, it will be all cleared up. Please wear a condom next time. When you find out which of your girly friends infected you, you better send her here."

He did believe his wife knew of his womanizing ways but she didn't seem to mind or acted like she didn't know. As long as he was sending money home she kept the issue out of their conversations. He had suspicions that she too was having an affair but could not confirm it.

By this time, it was his third year at Sacramento State and he's so busy with the band and dealing drugs that he finds himself with less motivation and time for school work and his grades began to show it.

Ronald Reagan is now governor and threatening to cut off funding for the program. With the money he was making he could easily survive and go on to graduate. He could afford a crew of "mules" to drive down to San Diego and pick up bigger loads of weed and pills; reds and whites, (barbiturates and amphetamine), and of course, there was always the coke.

Pips, his Sidro friend, would make loads of up to 150 kilos in the trunk of a rented LTD Ford. By now selling loads of that size were easy, with his new-found friends. More often now he would have to fly back to San Diego to pay the Tijuana drug dealers. Crossing the border with a grocery bag full of money, was also easier in those days, Mexican Customs did not care or just allowed it.

Things were moving fast. Then one night, at the Folsom Blvd., house while they were in one of the rooms weighing weed and counting pills, there was a knock at the door. When one of the band members opens the door, he's met with a gun to his face. Three masked men pushed themselves in and yelled for everyone to come into the living room and lay on the floor. Everyone did as they were told. These guys knew exactly where all the dope was. They took all the weed and pills and left. They were in a real hurry because they did not ask about money, of which he had a large stash in the house. It was a big setback, but he was able to pay off the debt to his people in Tijuana. School at this point became a second priority.

The following events proved to be a costly mistake on his part. It would affect his life in Sacramento and become the reason he doesn't graduate with a degree and possibly go on to Stanford. He had sent three of his crew to pick up 20 bricks of weed in San Diego, made the calls to his contacts in Tijuana and set the time and place for the pickup. The guys left and did not return as planned. He grew worried. Why were they taking so long to get back to Sacramento? Did they get arrested? Ripped off? Killed? When they finally showed up they tell him they had taken a detour to see some friends in Pomona who wanted some weed, so they decided to "front" three kilos to their friends. He was livid! They didn't have the money for the kilos but told him not to worry that their friends were trustworthy and would pay soon. They did not, and a war was brewing.

One Saturday afternoon around this same time his younger brother and two of his friends call and say they're in town. *"How do we get to your house?"* His brother and friends get to the house while the band is preparing to play at the club. They were only 19 years old, so he had to convince Sal..

> *"These guys are with me, my brother and his two friends are visiting me from San Diego, I'll be responsible for them,"* he tells him.

Sal was always wary of strangers in his club, but he agreed. His brother and friends were amazed at the operation he was running. They were more impressed, when a tall Filipina beauty with a lot of cleavage and wearing a mini skirt walks up to the table, bends over and plants a big wet kiss on his mouth. Lina had stayed at his house a couple of times, but they never really made it as a "couple." He always had this macho thing about women who were taller than him, but Lina was beautiful. The three Sidro vatos are totally impressed. Soon, talk of the three kilos that were never paid for, began. Someone tells his brother that one of the guys involved in the rip-off was sitting at the bar. It was Willy. To show what a badass he is his brother approaches Willy, tells him that he knows he had ripped-off his brother and proceeds to smash a lit cigarette into Willy's face. The "manager" was doing something else at the time and didn't see this until someone comes to tell him that his brother and Willy were outside fighting. He runs outside and there in the bushes was his brother and Willie scrapping it out. He grabs his brother, who had already done damage to Willie's face, Willie then runs off. Everything was cool back at the bar. The band played until closing. But they soon find out that Willy thinks he was *"jumped"* by both brothers.

The next day there was a free concert at one of the parks in Sacramento, so they decided to go hear the music. As the four arrive at the park, he spots Nancy, Willy's girlfriend sitting with some of her friends. He always had a crush on Nancy and envied Willy for having her though he knew she was madly in love with him. When he first arrived in Sacramento, Willy and he had become the best of friends, then Nancy came into their lives. The three of them were always together, hanging out at music bars and the park, dropping acid. They were quite a threesome. Then Willy and Nancy fall in love with each other. He still had a crush on her. To him she looked just like a 19-year-old Lauren Bacall, just gorgeous!

At the park that day, they chose a spot next to Nancy and her friends. She tells him that Willie is "really mad" at him for jumping and beating him up the night before.

"Jumped him?" He tells her that all he did was get his brother off of Willy.

> *"...Because my brother was beating the hell out of him."* She said he told the whole crew he was jumped and *"they are coming after you."*

He just ignored her. Suddenly they notice people starting to move away from the area where they were sitting. This alerted them and they get up off the grass to see guys coming at them from various angles. They cannot stand their ground because of all the punches they are receiving so they run off in different directions. He gets followed by Willy and two other guys who proceed to give him the beating of his life. Two punches from Willy to the face and he is down on the ground. As he is getting his ribs kicked he looks up to see who is the guy that is kicking him. It's Chai, a Felito! Somehow, he is not surprised. He always felt a kind of resentment and jealousy from Chai for the way their classmates treated him with high regard. He thinks of him as a kind of psychopath and the look on Chai's face that afternoon, as he is kicking him proves it. He's enjoying kicking the hell out of him.

His brother and friends meet at the car and begin driving around the park looking for him. They spot him running and pick him up.

"Where to?" they ask. He remembers Gloria, who now lives with his friend Richard. You could not find a mellower, nice guy. Richard knows the whole story about how Gloria was hurt by him. Gloria answers his knock on the door and gasps! He's a bloody mess. One eye is already closed, he has cuts to his face and his nose is bleeding.

"Who did this to you?" He tells her and Richard the story. As she's patching him up, he notices a tear in her eye and remembers how badly he had broken her heart just months earlier.

Theirs was mostly a one-way love affair—the kind where she came around on the nights he had no one else to share his bed with at the little one-bedroom house off Sacramento Blvd., across from General Hospital. Gloria would just show up knowing he was alone. She met him during the time she was going out with Willy, who met Nancy and dumped her. Gloria was a full-blooded Apache from the San Carlos reservation in Arizona. She was skinny and not particularly attractive with a scar under her left eye that she never quite explained. She was certainly not his type, but she was persistent—shy and quiet in person but fierce in bed. He really didn't know much about Gloria. She never even told him where she lived, and he didn't ask.

When they met, he still hadn't come to the level of drug dealing he was into now. Gloria would follow him around; tagging along uninvited, sometimes frustrating him. But she persisted and he gave in. While alone at night she would show up out of nowhere and he welcomed her to stay over. Together they smoked weed and listened to music like the Moody Blues, Santana and Van Morrison. Then it was off to bed! He had never been with a woman so powerful in bed. She taught him a lot about sex. Afterwards she would talk to him about her life on the reservation; how she was raised in poverty and the tricks her elders had shown her like how to properly stalk an animal, or even a human. When he asks about the stalking, she says something in her native tongue, and then explains in English that stalking is really about getting to know your territory. You stalk animals not to kill them but to see where they eat, what they eat, where they drink, even where they shit. You learn this so when you really need to kill one you will know how to hide, and you're able to eat. It's the same with humans, she says. Years later he will remember this conversation while training his staff in workforce development. The training topic today will be about the proper way of "Stalking Employers." He explains to his staff:

> *"To do effective job development for your clients, you must first learn how to stalk your targeted employer. You need to know in many ways what he/she eats, drinks, etc."*

He very much enjoyed their talks, with Gloria. He grew fond of her and she fell in love with him. He suspected once that she had used her powers to scare off another woman that he had met at Sac State. Laura had long jet-black hair and the body type he liked. After getting to know each other he invites Laura to his house. She is also Native American, part Cherokee. Soon Gloria becomes jealous.

> *"So, you got yourself another Indian girl huh?*
> *"How the hell do you know that?"*
> *"Cause I saw you two together. She's pretty, huh?"*
> *"Where, how, when did you see me?"*
> *"I made sure you did not see me."*
> *"You were stalking me?"*

She just smiles and walks away. He sees Laura a few more times and then suddenly she tells him that she wants to stop seeing him without an explanation. He suspects Gloria had something to do with it.

> *"Raven hair and ruby lips*
> *Sparks fly from her fingertips*
> *Echoed voices in the night*
> *She's a restless spirit on an endless flight*
> *Woo Hoo, witchy woman*
> *See how high she flies*
> *She got the moon in her eye*[8]

Gloria would often tell him that she loved him very much and that would annoy him.

> *"No! Do not do that, it will eventually come to hurt you!"*

She wouldn't listen to him, and when the Folsom Blvd. house was set up with the band, Gloria kept coming over. There were always different women at the house, groupies and other girlfriends. One day he had to tell Gloria not to come over anymore. She was hurt, and he felt bad. She never cried but he knew how bad he had hurt her and regretted it.

---

[8] *"Witchy Woman"* The Eagles 1972

"But it's too late to say you're sorry, how would I know, why should I care? Please don't bother trying to find her, she's not there."[9]

All that had come back to mind while Gloria was patching him up. When she finishes he thanks her and Richard, then leaves quickly. He remembers that he needs to get to the house as soon as possible. His stash of dope and money are there, and Willy and his crew are out for blood. He never sees Gloria again. He knows she will be alright. Richard seems to love her and he is the type of guy who will be successful in whatever endeavor he pursues. Gloria watches him leave through the window.

[9] *"She's Not There"* The Zombies 1965

11

CHASED OUT OF SACRAMENTO

Back at the house while he's packing his stuff a call comes in. Its Willy saying that if they don't get out of that house and completely out of Sacramento they will come in shooting. He knows all too well how well-armed they are and all he has is a little .25 caliber semi-automatic hand gun. It would have been his last and deadly mistake to have a shoot out there at the house. He was told that if he left peacefully no one else would get hurt, and that they were going to be followed out of town to make sure they were gone. He quickly packs up some clothes, grabs $8,000 in cash and a couple of kilos of weed. He leaves a lot of other personal things behind and that's the last he will see of the Folsom house. The band would ultimately have a hard time keeping the house, so he calls Freddie and tells him they can sell the furniture.

"Good luck. I'm outta here!"

Sure, enough when he walks outside they were waiting for him. He loads up the car with what he can and his brother and friends follow behind him. With two other cars following behind them, they leave town. Willy and his crew followed for about an hour out of Sacramento and then turned around. Once they get to Stockton they rented two rooms at a motel where they would lick their wounds and rest. He called his wife to tell her what happened and asks her to begin looking for a house to rent. But Sacramento wasn't done with him yet. He has never been a vengeful person and didn't think of getting payback from those guys but his brother and friends wanted to.

> *"We can put a crew together in San Diego and come back to take them out."*

He was against the plan, too much of a risk that could end up costing him.

> *"Dump that plan,"* he said.

When he gets home his wife just shakes her head when she sees him. She is very mad. His mother-in-law bandages him up. They are able to find a house on Oxford Street in Chula Vista to rent and he starts making plans for what's next.

He could keep dealing with his white friends Bob and Nate who live in North Sacramento. They have two different networks that he could use to expand his market. Cocaine was their drug of choice, which meant he didn't have to deal with the bulky weed.

Back in San Ysidro he was amazed at how many of his homeboys had gotten into the business and were moving big loads. They began making some serious money for themselves but especially for their suppliers. He soon learned that most of them had moved to Chula Vista and didn't want to operate out of Sidro because it would be too dangerous for their families. It became so popular that Chula Vista started to jokingly be called "Culiacansito" or little Culiacan, Sinaloa, where the big Mexican dealers were beginning to make their turf. Most of our dope was coming from there and this was surely the start of what are now "The Mexican Cartels."

He begins to hang out more in Tijuana. The bars along Avenida Revolucion were the hotbed of dope dealers. There was Mike's Bar, The Aloha and The Long Bar to name just a few. At one of these bars across the street from the Jai Alai is where for the first time, he gets his jaw broken in a fight. He was so drunk he blacked out and would not remember much of what led up to it, but it was probably over a woman because the guy who knocked him out was a friend of his who had a beautiful girlfriend. She was one of three sisters of his main weed supplier at the time. They were from Culiacan and carried what would become a very famous last name among drug dealers in Tijuana.

He ended up in a hospital that night across the street from the racetrack and as soon as he regained consciousness, he called his compadre Julian to come and pick him up. Julian came over in the morning and took him to Mercy Hospital in San Diego where his mouth was wired shut for 11 weeks. It was a good thing that his front lower tooth was knocked out. It made it easy to squeeze soft food past the wires.

After healing from the broken jaw he needed to get back to work and as Rod Stuart would sing *"or find myself a rock and roll band – that needs a helping hand."* Well, it was obvious to him now that if you look hard enough you will find what you are looking for. A friend knew of a startup band and would introduce him. He meets the guys and immediately likes all of them. They had been playing hard rock covers and did not yet have a name. He suggested the name *"Aztlan"* the mythical home of the Aztecs or the *"Mexica"* people. Aztlan is also an important Chicano Movement symbol. The band members were all Chicanos and really liked the name, so they adopted it. He gives them his proposition—the same plan he had had for East-West. They liked the plan.

They were all good musicians and it did not take long before they needed a gig to play. He gets to work and chooses a bar in National City located on what was called "The Mile of Bars" the area at the corner of National Avenue and 8th Avenue. In the '70s the block was lined with strip joints and night clubs. Sailors from the nearby Navy base filled the establishments and he thought it would be a great place to do business. He spoke to the owner who agreed to audition the band. Aztlan got the gig to play three nights a week.

Business was going well but he and his wife weren't getting along—arguments were getting violent and she would run home to her mother. During that time, he met a girl named Janet and began spending more time with her. Eventually they moved in together. He was now doing more business in amphetamines. David, his connection for pills, stashed the drugs in bags under the dashboard of a car. At the club the band began to bring in more customers. Truckers, sailors and others needed a lift from downers and booze, so whites were in big demand.

At some point his wife found out where the band was playing and decided to confront him and Janet one night. She comes into the club, searches him out and sees Janet and him sitting at a table. She waits until Janet gets up to go to the bathroom and follows her in. Not long after the manager rushes over to him screaming that Janet and a woman are fighting in the women's bathroom. They go in and hear the commotion. He opens a stall door to see his wife pummeling Janet with punches. He grabs her and takes her outside and is holding her arms to try and stop her from hitting him. Someone called the police, and while the argument was going on outside a cop comes at him with his baton. As the officer lifts the baton his wife stops him.

"I'm his wife and I will be the one to beat the shit out of him!"

The cop could see now what was really going on.

"Officer, may I take my wife home?"
"OK, but no more trouble."

At that time, he was driving a little beauty of a 1964 red convertible Ford Mustang. As they're headed down 8ᵗʰ Avenue and under the Interstate 5 freeway bridge, she begins to try and kick out the windshield of his car. By luck it doesn't shatter. He throws it in the backseat and heads south on the freeway. The cold wind in her face calms her down. He doesn't know how Janet managed to get home, but the club owner told him later that she was well beaten in the face. Over the phone she tells him she doesn't want to see him anymore. *"Too much drama!"*

12

"A COCAINE DEALER"

He keeps working the club. His friend Ted, the gentle giant, is a massive guy but a real sweetheart. Ted alone was taking all the shipments of whites. Ted was a trucker/mechanic who had a good market in his business and could be trusted. Even now, when, occasionally traveling the 125 North he can see Ted's old house from the freeway and the memories of how much merchandise he unloaded at that house still amazes him.

He soon began getting calls from his two white friends in Sacramento. They needed coke! He gets a pound and a half "fronted" to him, he hides 2 ounces in each of his boots he is wearing and 12 ounces in his guitar and case. He must go through three major air ports; San Diego, Los Angeles and Sacramento. He completes this first drug-running trip without problems. Tom picks him up at the airport in Sacramento.

"Hey man, you OK? I couldn't do that shit. I'd be too damn nervous."

"Naw man, everybody thinks I'm a wanna-be rock star, and way too obvious to be carrying dope."

Nate was a clean-cut all-American kid from a well-to-do family in North Sacramento and had cash handy to pay on delivery. With Tom he had to work with him to cut the coke into gram's and ounces.. Tom was a scraggly long-haired guy with glasses and could be counted on for delivery. He held a black belt in Karate, which was a bonus. Nate on the other hand was ruthless. One day while delivering cocaine, he spots Chai on the road, reminding Nate of Chai's involvement with his old Sacramento crew and how he was chased out of town.

"You wanna do him? I'm packing." Nate says.

"Are you out of your fucking mind? We're on business here!"
He yells at Nate

He sensed that Nate was annoyed that he didn't seek revenge so easily. He tells Nate to drive on. He didn't want Chai to know that he was back in town.

"If you want to blow that fucker away, do it later and not around me."

On the next trip, he is with Miguel, his long-time friend from Palm City. Miguel had four kilos of coke that needed to be unloaded quickly. He tells Miguel that if he wants a fast turnover they could drive to Sacramento, give half of them to Nate and he could be on a plane back home that same day with extra money in his pocket for the drop off. He would stay with Tom to piece out the other two kilos.

The plan was set, and they take off for Sacramento in the VW. It was a 9-hour ride. They had stashed the four kilos in the door panels of the VW. They're stopped at the San Onofre Border Patrol checkpoint. They were acting nervous, so the officer tells them to get out of the car. He shines his flashlight in and flips up the back door of the station wagon. Satisfied, the Border Patrol officer tells them to get on their way. They pull over at the first Denny's restaurant they see in San Clemente to grab some coffee. But as Miguel was getting out of the car one of the kilos on his side falls to the ground in the parking lot. They just stared at each other in disbelief and then began laughing their heads off like two little kids.

Close to Sacramento they stop to call Nate.

"Get the cash ready for the two keys, because "I have to put my friend on a plane ASAP." "Yeah man," he said.

Upon arrival Nate is true to his word. He pays him off and takes Miguel to the airport with his cash. Miguel is a very happy dude.

Getting back to the city he calls Tom who rushes over and gives him a big hug.

"Good to see you man!"

Tom tells him in order to get the most money out of the merchandise; it would maybe take two to three months to sell in ounces and grams. Tom tells him that his wife Gail has a friend with a safe house and that he's already talked with Robin and paid her cash just for the day. Tom has another safe house elsewhere. Robin lives with her 3-year-old son. At the house Gail and Robin are waiting for them. He already knew Gail, so he is introduced to Robin. She is about 5 foot 7 inches and 125 pounds with gorgeous lips and hazel eyes that looked very Mediterranean. She seemed to be a very intelligent and a sharp-witted woman.

It was mid afternoon and they sat down in the kitchen to make plans and test out the merchandise. They discussed how and in what amounts they should cut the coke, who to go to first and where they would stash it. Tom made a few calls then they sit down to snort a little coke and drink beer.

Later that night he had to use the bathroom, which meant he had to go through Robin's bedroom. He gently knocked on the door, peeked in and announced that he needed to use the bathroom. She points and says, "Right through there." As he is walking past her bed, he's stopped cold in his tracks by her legs. She's lying on her bed wearing short little undies and as he looks up to her, she giggles and says "hi." He goes over to her side of the bed and the romance takes off like a bullet. In the morning while they're showering, she turns to him.

"Never in my wildest dreams would I have ever imagined that I would someday be showering with a cocaine dealer."

He takes her from behind, *"You have now babe."*

The next day, he catches up with Tom to apologize for the night before, leaving him in the kitchen.

> *"Don't worry about it," he said. "My wife and I knew that something like that would happen."*

Business took off rapidly and his love affair with Robin was going great. They ate dinner out almost every night, went clubbing and got high. She wasn't too much into cocaine, just weed. Then one afternoon while they're making love a call comes in. Robin answers and he could hear a woman's angry voice on the other end. Robin listened quietly and then speaks in a sexy voice.

> *"Yes he's in. In fact, about a minute ago he was all the way in."*
> She then lets out a sexy moan.

Oh my god! It couldn't be! My wife? How did she get this number? He grabs the phone from Robin and his wife begins giving him hell. *"You better get your ass home now!"* Bob calls shortly after.

> *"Hey man, your wife called me to say that she needed to talk to you because of some emergency, so I had to give her Robin's number."*

Not too smart on Tom's part. Now he's in trouble with the wife again. She must have gotten Bob's number through the phone bill.

He couldn't just leave and drop everything in the middle of the business. Besides his car was in the shop—after all the abuse and miles he'd put it through it needed some major servicing. In a few days he's ready to take the trip back home. Robin was furious.

> *"How long will you be gone?"*
> *"Not sure."* he replies.

He takes the plane back home just to catch more hell—a dumb thing to do but he had no choice. Besides, he was failing in his responsibilities to his family. His calls to Robin begin to take a bad turn. She becomes furious that he would likely not return as soon as she expected him to.

"*What about your car?*" she asks.
"*Well I will have to go and pick it up sometime soon.*"

In a few days he calls her again. She tells him to forget about his car since the bank had repossessed it.

"*I told them where they could find it.*"
"*Why did you do that?*"
"*Because you're a big fucking liar!*"
And she hangs up on him.

Sure-enough when he called the bank, they told him that because of non-payment the car was repossessed. There goes the car and now he has to get a new car. Robin got her payback. He would never see her again.

He was getting tired of traveling to Sacramento so frequently and on each trip, he begins to use coke more and more. One night at a friend's house he's sitting on the floor with his back to the wall. He starts nodding off and then suddenly begins to see a kaleidoscope of colors—the kind of colors he would see when he would drop acid. His body is shivering and jerking about, and the wife of the friend comes over to shake him from his state. In the last three days he had not slept much and had eaten very little with mostly just cocaine in his system.

"*Hey what's the matter with you? Have you eaten anything? Have you slept? You look terrible man. Your body was shaking, it scared us.*"

He barely replies.

"*Come on let me fix you some soup.*"

She heats up a can of soup and serves it to him. His hand is shaking so badly that he hardly put the spoon in his mouth so she helps feed him, like a baby! He starts feeling better but begins to have paranoid thoughts.

> *"Am I dying? I must wait for Tom to pay me off so I can go home. He's taking too long. Did he rip me off? What if these people are planning to do something to me?"*

He knows he's panicking and needs to sleep and stay away from the coke. He finally nods off to sleep and is awakened hours later. Tom is there with the money.

> *"Man, I was really paranoid last night! Gotta stop doing so much coke!"*

He thanks his friend and gets on the first plane to San Diego.

For the next two sales he has Nate comes down to San Diego for the coke. He works at mending things with his wife again. He wasn't going back to Sacramento anytime soon.

13

CHULA VISTA

In Chula Vista, a group of his long-time friends from San Ysidro hung out at a place called Victor's II. It's a spacious, classy place with a lot of pool tables. Here, none of the dealers are armed. It wasn't like Sacramento where there were turf wars between crews. To them the entire South Bay was their turf. No one bothered each other. It was late 1973 and things were not all that bad, yet.

His contacts across the border wanted him to move bigger loads of weed. It made him wonder, *how in the hell are they getting so much weed across the border? Just driving it on through?* He was still too naïve to think that the weed was let through by corrupt customs officers being paid hundreds of thousands of dollars by drug dealers in Mexico.

The huge loads were good if he had the customers. He begins with 250 kilo loads that would be driven across the border in a 1969-70 Ford LTD. The driver would park the Ford in a public parking spot downtown, leave the keys and parking ticket on top of one of the tires and he would have to be there as soon as they signaled him to. At this point he realized he now needs a bigger house. The house where they lived on Oxford Street in Chula Vista has no garage.

The couple goes house shopping and finds a 3-bedroom with a large garage in a housing tract near Southwestern Community College, a nice neighborhood where everyone appeared to mind their own business. Trees and the way the house was situated assured privacy. There were no houses across the street facing theirs. They moved in and he begins bringing in the loads. All he has to do it is back the Ford into the garage and close the door. No more public parking lots. He had to move the weed fast and he only had two customers that could handle loads of that size.

Rafael, his movement brother and old friend, is going to school at UCLA. Rafael and a friend make regular trips to the house to return to school with a decent load of weed. Another friend Luis, who he met at a bar in Tijuana, has a good market in National City.

One night as he and his friend Pips were weighing out some coke, his wife comes running into the room yelling that someone was in the backyard trying to get into the house. He doesn't hear barking from Tino, their 3-year old Shepherd mix.

> *"Stash everything and don't make a sound until you hear from me,"* he tells Pips. *"If anyone comes through that door that's not me, fuck him up."*

> *"OK"* he says.

He runs down the hall to the bedroom to get his gun from the closet and as he comes out gun pointed, he sees a person enter through the back door. At the same moment his 4-year-old son, who had followed him, is now in the middle of the hallway pointing his toy pistol at the intruder. He now knows who the intruder is, low-life Jorge, and his brothers' friend:

> *"Jorge! Stop, can't you see my son there? I am dropping my gun."*

The wife runs to pick up the boy and the two men go into the kitchen, he is now unarmed.

> *"What the fuck is all this about"* he yells at Jorge.

"*You won't front us any coke, you sold out La Raza and even your own brother. So now I came to get the coke myself.*"

"*First off, how the hell do you know where I even live? And how do you know if I have any coke now? Drop the gun let's you and I go outside*" he dares him.

His wife comes running into the kitchen mad as hell and she begins to scold Jorge, like he was her child. Jorge still has the gun on him and his wife moves between them. Jorge gently tries to move her away by gently placing his hand right above her breast. She didn't even try to move his hand away as if it had not been the first time his hand had touched her there. He has a strange gut feeling but holds his anger for the time being. She is really yelling at Jorge now. He moves back, then out the door and is gone. Pips comes running in.

"*What the hell was all that about?*"

He tells his friend what had just happened but can't confront his wife with his suspicions because Pips is there.

"*Hey bro, let's go back and finish packaging the coke.*"

Pips is concerned about how mad he is and he tries to calm him down, asking questions about the whole incident. He doesn't want to talk about it and tells Pips to forget it.

Both his brother and bother-in-law had been hanging out with Jorge from San Ysidro for some time. They would hang out in the garage, of their mom's house where his wife and son were living. Whenever he was home from school in Sacramento, on vacation or back from delivering drugs, he would hang out with them too. At first Jorge was not really into drugs but later began using more until he was known as a regular "druggie." He earned the reputation as a real lowlife.

When he moved his family into the new house he was aware that Jorge and his brother were roommates. They lived a rundown apartment somewhere in National City. He certainly did not want either of them to know where he lived now. Whenever he would run into his brother, his brother would pester him to front him some coke. He told him to forget about it, that he knew what the consequences would be, and he would never get paid. This is business; he tells his brother *"nothing to do with family"*.

The next day he thinks hard about what went down the night before. He is very mad.

> *"Why didn't Tino bark? He is a great watch dog. How did Jorge know where I lived? How did he even know how to get in the side gate?"*

He is thinking more clearly now, and as he thinks he thumps his forehead hard.

> *"You big Pendejo you! You asshole! He had to have been in your house before. All those nights you were out screwing around with other women, dealing or whatever, this fuck must have had a grand time with your wife!"*

He thinks some more. Confront his wife? Start a big fight? He knows that all this is just plain payback. He has too much going on right now to get into it with his wife.

The matter did not come up because she did all she could to avoid the subject.

> *"Jorge is an asshole and not worth you getting into trouble over him."*
> His wife would tell him.

He knew it was time to find another house. About two months later he gets the news that Jorge had drowned and died while swimming at the south end of Imperial Beach. The fool was surely very stoned on something and tried to go swimming. So that was the end of that. I did not see my brother again for some time and he did not get his revenge on that sorry bastard, Jorge!

The house near the college had worked out well but they would have to move. Sooner or later someone would notice, and he shouldn't get too confident. Back to house hunting. He finds the house he was looking for right in the middle of Chula Vista on Dennis Street by an elementary school. It's an older house on a corner lot in a quiet neighborhood with a big yard and three bedrooms. The old garage was not attached to the house but faced the side street with no other houses in front of it. It was perfect. The trunk loads of marijuana continue to arrive.

Soon he starts inviting some heads of the other crews, working the heavy loads, to come over and chat over dinner. He wants to know more about how the other crews are operating. First to come over was Papa Louie with his brother and a couple of guys from his crew. Papa Louie learned about moving the large loads he is now moving and is impressed enough to come over and chat. Of interest to Louie was whether my connections are in anyway related to his. It seems that most guys dealing out of Tijuana at the time were either from Culiacan Sinaloa or the State of Jalisco. There seems to be a real sense of trouble ahead. In Tijuana, they know a turf war is about to explode. They couldn't really identify what it was, but it was looming.

After close to a year of living there he discovered his neighbor was a ranking officer of the Chula Vista Police Department. He was always in "plain clothes" and did not drive a patrol car. One nice Sunday afternoon he's outside mowing his lawn and the neighbor comes over to say hi. They introduce themselves and he sees the badge on his neighbors' belt. The neighbor is standing next to the curb right in front of an LTD Ford loaded with weed. He tells the neighbor that he is in the roofing business. He has pop's old Chevy pickup, which fronted well as a roofer's truck and he happened to do some roofing while he lived there. Still, having a cop for a neighbor was just too dumb to keep the business coming out of the house. He is now working more with Rafael and Randy. He tells them about the neighbor and that they need to find another house.

They find a house on Alabama Street in Imperial Beach, just north of Palm Avenue. The house had the right details they wanted. This is where Randy and his girlfriend would live and receive loads of weed. On one occasion a big tomato truck came to drop of a 500-kilo load of weed hidden behind tomato crates.

> *"What the hell am I supposed to do with all these tomatoes?"*
> He asks the dealer.

> *"Whatever you want to do with them, sell them or something, we don't care"* was their response.

So, for each load that went out the buyer would get a few crates of tomatoes. It was like getting green stamps at the grocery store. During times of heavy load deliveries, his crew had to stay at the house until all the merchandise was sold.

14

PAT

He doesn't remember how or who introduced him to Pat, but Pat was a piece of work. An elderly lady maybe in her mid-60s', she had connections to move tons of weed. She gives him what he has been looking for—a single customer that could take care of all his loads. Now he doesn't have to look anywhere else and expose himself foolishly. What luck! She could pass as his grandmother or aunt. She was regularly seen at the house, in Chula Vista, staying over a couple of nights at a time to appear like she was family. She would come down from Dana Point with her son-in-law Ray, who helped her make the runs back and forth. They moved a lot of weed and on a couple of occasions she would even go to Tijuana and bring coke across in her girdle. Who would suspect a little old lady with a piñata holding a pound of coke in her undies? She was smart and only did a few trips before she stopped. She had all the weed she needed and a perfect set up with him in Chula Vista. Why ruin it?

On the last night he ever sees Pat again; they spend a late night together, getting high, son-in-law Ray is also there chatting. Later his wife retires to their bedroom and goes to sleep. Pat's son-in-law is in the dining room where he usually spreads out a sleeping bag. Pat and he go into the guest room to do some coke. She begins to tell him what a perfect thing they have going and if given the chance she would make him very rich and they could be on top of the world together in Dana Point! He couldn't believe his ears. Then she moves over to the floor, kneels between his legs, pulls them apart and begins to unzip his pants. Just then Ray walks past the open door as he heads for the bathroom and sees dear old mom-in-law on her knees in front of him. She hears Ray approaching and couldn't get up fast enough. Ray just continued to the bathroom, like he had not seen anything. He never, ever would have imagined what this lady was up to. She was certainly too old for him. He didn't even know if he could get it up for her.

In the morning they packed 150 kilos of weed and headed out with not one word spoken about the night before. He didn't know it yet but that would be the last time he would ever see Pat again. Pat usually called him when they would get back to Dana Point. This time there is no call. He's getting worried, so he calls the number to her house and her daughter answers.

> *"This morning Mom and Ray got busted in San Onofre. Ray told me that the law was just sitting there waiting for them to drive up. They knew exactly what was in the car. They must have been fingered."*

Now he is really scared. He tells his wife to go to her mom's house and that they would need to find another place to live.

> *"Who fingered the load? And why did they not come after me and raid the house? Am I being saved for something else? I can't be that lucky!"*

Things were getting too weird. His supplier during this time was a guy nicknamed Bull, a big, fat young Mexican, not yet in his 30s. Bull also disappears, and he later finds out that Bull's remains were found in two 50-gallon barrels. His remains probably waiting on the *"Pozolero"* (The Stewmaker) to do his hideous duty;

> *"Eight years have passed since the day Mexican authorities detained a man named Santiago Meza Lopez. At that time, President Felipe Calderon's administration began referring to Meza as **El Pozolero de Tijuana** ("The Stewmaker"), a reference to the fact that he was believed to have dissolved some 300 people in caustic soda"*[10]

---

[10] Vice News, Dec 7, 2017

He is now running scared. He decides to look up some of his old Movement friends at San Diego State and stays with them for a while. He doesn't know what to do next.

> *"Against the Wind* We *were running against the wind*
> *we were young and strong*
> *We were running against the wind*
> *Guess I lost my way there were oh so many roads*
> *I was livin' to run and running to live*
> *Never worried about payin' or even how much I owe"*[11]

It's now 1975 and a lot of people are getting busted. He needs a new life. They rent a little house in North Park and he brings his family in. He starts roofing again but needs something more stable. Roofing is seasonal, even in San Diego's beautiful weather.

---

[11] Against the wind, Bob Seger and the Silver Bullet Band 1980

15

THE VIDA HOUSE

One of his old movement friends Frank has some ideas about building a half-way house for young heroin addicts. Frank was also quite a character; an ex-con who was intelligent and an excellent public speaker. But he was also a heroin addict. One night he is over at Frank's house. His wife Moyra is also there—the woman who would become his second wife a few years after Frank passes away. Frank shows him the proposal he had written for the rehab home. It would be called VIDA (Viable Innovative Drug Alternatives), but it needed funding. He's very impressed with Frank's work. Frank takes the proposal to present at different community groups. It always amazed him to see how easy it was for Frank to speak in front of large groups. On many occasions he would have the group applauding with standing ovations.

The MAAC Project (Mexican-American Advisory Council) applied to the County of San Diego and received funding for the VIDA House. Frank, who would be the director, wanted him to be on the counseling staff. The House was established at the corner of National Avenue and 2nd Avenue across the street from the old Keith's Restaurant and up the street where Aztlan played their gigs on the Mile of Bars.

VIDA was founded as a co-ed heroin addicts living center. The program survived only because of MAAC's leadership. A psychologist would come regularly to hold therapy groups, which seemed to help the residents, but it was soon learned that real help would need to come from the inside. In other words, staff needed training in drug counseling and group therapy. Once during group, he spotted the good psychologist with a covered pistol in his waistband. He could not believe it! Following a session with MAAC leadership staff the psychologist's contract was terminated.

Frank didn't last long as a director. His heroin addiction was too strong and MAAC fired him. Two other directors came and went as well. The VIDA program was moved to the 2nd Avenue building in 1979. The following year a bulletin had been received from the University of Florida announcing the recruitment of bilingual counseling staff for the Cuban refugee program. During the Carter Administration the President allowed some 125,000 "Marielito's" from Cuba to come into the U.S. The program needed personnel to provide logistics for such a large project.

"On Tuesday, April 3, 1980, six Cubans crashed through the gate of the Peruvian Embassy in Havana seeking political asylum. During the incident a Cuban policeman was killed, and the Castro government removed the remainder of the guard in presumed retaliation. Within fort-eight hours, over ten thousand Cubans had sought asylum in the unprotected embassy and perhaps as many as 100,000 had congregated in the areas adjacent to the site, hoping to find means to enter. Thus, began a new Cuban exodus. On April 23, Fidel Castro opened the door to a migration of unprecedented proportions."[12]

---

[12] **The Heritage Foundation** report **The Cuban Refugee Problem in Perspective 1959 - 1980**

16

THE "GAP"

The money from VIDA was not enough. He was getting paid something like $900 a month. In looking forward another job, he found that The Cuban Refugee Project was paying $1,500 a month and would provide a room at a nearby motel and a car. He called the recruiters and gave them a short history of his counseling career in the past three years working with young adults with criminal records and drug addictions. They hired him on the spot and sent him a plane ticket to Harrisburg, PA. The program assigned him to Fort Indiantown Gap, an old WWII Army base where they housed the Cuban minors while they were being processed for "sponsorship" to families in the states. An orientation was held for the newcomers, in which the program was outlined along with the chain of command, the history was explained, expected duties and behaviors were given and how salary payments were processed. They were then assigned rooms at a nearby motel. The counselors are teamed up by their home state and his new roommate will be Rafael; a tall happy guy with curly hair. Rafael is from San Jose, California and could easily be a lineman for any football team. They settle into their new home and are soon taken to the "Gap." On their way they pass by the Penn National Race Track for thoroughbred horseracing. As they drive by memories flash across his mind, specifically the way he would joke and tell people how he was literally raised under a horse's ass.

Barracks similar to the ones at the "Gap"

The program proved to be a real adventure for him. Each counselor was assigned a barracks with up to 25 Cuban kids in each. There were six rows of barracks and in the middle they are separated by chain-link fence, with boys on one side, girls on another.. The Cuban youth liked the Chicano staff, but they had problems getting along with the Puerto Rican staff. Chicanos on staff could not figure out why their Puerto Rican coworkers were not liked by the Cubans, and would pull pranks on them.

The Cuban kids like the counselor from San Diego; and nicknamed him "*San Diego.*" One night, while working the overnight sift, in the barracks there was a lot of joking and laughing that went late into the evening. He got tired of all the noise and mischief that from the front door of the barrack yells out:

> "*Ya no esten Chingando tanto, todos a dormir!*" *Stop fucking around and go to sleep!*

At hearing this from him, the kids busted out laughing again. He did not know that the word "Chingando" to the Cuban's actually means having sex.

The night shift had the duty of keeping order in the camp, which was no easy task. There were always fights. One of their biggest problems was keeping the gay Cuban kids safe from the rest of the population. Those poor kids were assaulted and raped almost nightly. One night the staff found a gay kid inside a locker that belonged to an older Cuban youth. This older kid would hide the younger kid in his locker during the day and at night take him out and rape him at his pleasure. I wondered how the hell he was able to keep it from the counselor assigned to that barrack. At night the administration would show movies and do their best to keep the kids entertained. But stuff happened all the time. After a kid was stabbed in a fight, staff found out that knives were being made right there in camp. So, a "knife patrol" was set up by staff to search all barracks and that's how the young Cuban kid was found in the locker. Kids caught making these offenses would be taken out of the camp and placed in a prison facility.

Not long after arriving at the camp he notices a woman paying special attention to him. Her name is Melissa, a sexy looking Chicana from San Antonio, Texas. They began seeing each other regularly and they had to find a way to have a more intimate rendezvous. It was arranged one night that Melissa's roommate would be out for the night, they both wanted to spend the night together. They made love and he stayed for the night. From there on a strong romance began, Rafael, his roommate did not even approach the idea of their relationship; he felt a bit of jealousy from Raphael.

Staff received word that the Gap would close for the coming winter and the need to "sponsor off" kids was urgent. Sponsoring a kid entailed an American family applying for eligibility and upon approval the sponsoring family would take the kid in as family with adoption being optional. But many issues soon arose because of the hasty way the program was developed. Staff learned that some kids ended up practically working as slaves on a farm somewhere with too much follow-up needed to assure the kids were not abused in any way, and it appeared that the program did not have the resources for that kind of follow-up service.

He and his kids were saddened because their adventure was coming to an end. On the last night he slept at the camp in a station that was set up for overnight staff. In the morning when he wakes up, he feels hard objects under his pillow. When he looks under the pillow, he finds four homemade knives!

>*"Wow! What is the message here? And how did they get four knives under my pillow without waking me?"*

He is very concerned and seeks help from his lead supervisor.

>*"I think it is a compliment! They like you and did that as a sort of going away present. I don't know of any other counselor who was given knives in that way. It's just their way of showing how much they appreciated you; don't take it like a threat."*

At the gate that night, as the kids are being loaded into the busses, some of the kids turned over their knives, and it seemed to everyone that they were showing staff who was smarter. He goes over to the officer at the gate and in front of everyone hands over the knives. The officer is impressed.

>*"How did you find so many in such a short time?"*

>*"They were under my pillow when I woke up this morning."*

>*"What? Are you okay?"*

>*"Yeah my boss told me they were given to me as a present out of respect."*

The officer shakes his head. Many of the kids in line to board the busses saw what happened and passed the word on to his kids who were already on the bus.

That night the camp is cleared and he walks the empty barrack. Though it had only been four-month assignment bittersweet memories engulf him. He thinks of "his kids" and wishes the very best for them.

In the morning there is a lot of talk about where to go next. Luckily there weren't a lack of options. He is asked to join the *"Vision Quest"* program out of Tucson, Arizona. Members of that organization were very interested in signing him up. They liked the counselor from San Diego and knew he was an experienced ranch-hand who could ride a horse.

"How do you know all that?" he asks,

"The kids from your barracks told our Vision Quest counselors about the stories you would tell them of growing up in a ranch when you were young. Are those stories true?"

"Of course, they're true. Man, who goes around making up stories like that?"

"Well we sure could use a guy like you on the Wagon Train. Will you sign up?"

"Let me get back to you. I've got to talk it over with Melissa first."

The kids in his barrack were very interested in what their counselor's life was like in the states. They would ask him questions about his childhood. One night he decides to tell them a story of his life as a young boy. The kids would eagerly crowd around him to hear of his upbringing in the horse ranches of San Ysidro. They loved the stories so much that it became a nightly ritual before bed.

The Wagon Train program would be a six-month trek. Twenty-five Cuban youth were selected to go through the Vision Quest program, upon arrival in Tucson; they would live on the program grounds, get an education and have an opportunity for citizenship. He would be given a horse with all the gear and would travel from Harrisburg to Tucson. Better pay and back on a saddle. What an offer! The Vision Quest administrators did all they could to convince him to sign on. He tells Melissa about the offer.

"Are you crazy? You are going to give up a cozy apartment with me to go out into the wilderness, act like Davy Crocket, get bitten by bugs and sleep out in the middle of nowhere?!" she tells him.

He goes back to tell the Vision Quest people that he will not be signing up.

His love affair with Melissa was in full swing. She has signed up to work in Washington D.C. at the St. Elizabeth's Hospital (the St. Elsewhere of television fame). He doesn't think twice about it and signs up for the D.C. assignment. In the near future, he will realize what a big mistake this turns out to be, but he is totally into his love affair with Melissa and doesn't look back. They are given a nice apartment in Alexandria, Va. and they move in together. Melissa has a college degree and is given a supervisory position at the hospital; he is assigned a counselor position in the mental health ward. Adult men suffering from various forms of severe mental illnesses are his charges. He had never worked with folks like this before and he felt much unprepared. It didn't take long for him to become dissatisfied with the job and he soon regrets not taking the Vision Quest job offer.

One morning as he is making his rounds in the ward, he hears shouting, screams and furniture being thrown about. He runs into one of the big rooms and sees several men fighting, breaking furniture and windows with staff running in all directions. Then a fire breaks out in one of the rooms. He goes into another room and sees a man on the floor with a broken glass in his hands ready to cut his wrist. He enters the room slowly, gets on the floor and begins to talk to him, begging the man to put down the glass.

"No!" the man screams as he slashes his wrist.

> *"Vete, Vete de aqui dejame morir!"* *Get out of here let me die!*
> The man screams.

Now he hears even more commotion, sees smoke and people rushing out. He's told to leave immediately. Everyone else is already out. He makes his way to the entrance passing by people who are crying, yelling and cursing. He peaks out the front door and sees a line of police officers who are aiming their guns at the front entrance, where he plans to exit. All he has is his ID on a lanyard. *Will the police know I am not Cuban, and not shoot me?* The helicopters overhead are making too much noise for the cops to hear people identifying themselves. Anything could go wrong. With his ID in one hand and the other up in the air he steps out. Melissa is running toward the frontline waving not to shoot. They let him pass. He realizes he's just survived a violent riot at St. Elizabeth's Hospital.[13] They had been on the job for less than two months and are now to be assigned to Prairie du Chien in Wisconsin at a Cuban Youth boy's camp.

---

[13] This incident was never reported by the major media outlets

17

PRAIRIE DU CHIEN

They fly to La Crosse, Wisconsin where they're picked up by the camp's director, none other than Raphael, his old roommate at the "Gap." They were happy to see a familiar face. After all that had happened to them months and weeks seemed like years.

"So how did you manage to make Camp Director? Must pay good huh?"

Man! I have a degree, don't you remember? I also have good connections and it's about "who you know" that counts, and yeah, the pay is much better. Let's party!" Rafael responds.

The program has rented some apartments in town, and he and Melissa were assigned a room. It's winter now and for southerners like them it was too damned cold! They still had a little celebration with Raphael, swapped war stories and then it was off to bed.

The camp is made up of several cabins with no fences. There are up to five boys in each cabin, all of who came from the Gap, so the couple knows them well. Raphael always had a crush on Melissa and there were feelings of jealousy back at the Gap when his roommate ends up getting the girl. And now that he will be her boss it's even more valuable to him. They are assigned cabins and get to work with the boys. It seemed to him that the rules were too lenient, leaving too much room for mischief.

He doesn't call home very often during those days, only to tell his wife that he had just sent money home. She doesn't nag or scold him about it; she doesn't even bring it up. She doesn't sound very lonely either and he suspects that she's not alone.

Just a week into their assignment and in the middle of the night they receive a call from camp. Some boys had escaped their camp that night, broke into a nearby house, stolen bottles of liquor and a .22mm rifle. At around midnight he and Melissa are called to the camp to provide aid. It's snowing and windy, a miserable night! They get to the camp and Esteban, another veteran of the Gap, is there also. Esteban is a Chicano from Chicago.

> *"You two know those kids, I think you guys could go in there and talk them into coming out,"* Raphael says.

Both counselors look at each other. They know the kids are armed and by now very drunk. Are we crazy? In the snow at one in the morning they creep up to the cabin, peak in and begin to talk to the boys inside, who were so drunk it seemed they had forgotten what trouble they were in. They are invited to party with them. Both counselors slowly enter the cabin and spot the .22 against the wall.

> *"Oye Chicano's pasenle, como dicen ustedes – a pistiar?"*
> *(Hey Chicanos, come on in and drink with us)*
>
> *"Orale, dame la botella"*

They grab a bottle and sit on the floor with them. Then the counselors begin.

> *"OK, Ya vamos a salir, no va ver problemas, si no salimos ahorita va a ver policias afuera."* (OK we are going to go outside. If we don't leave now, there will be many policemen outside and many troubles for all of you") "Ok vamos!"

And they begin for the door. Esteban peaks out and sees a line of police officers pointing weapons at the cabin. He gets a flashback to St. Elizabeth's. "Not again!" Raphael is now at the frontline assuring the officers that his staff has just ended the incident peacefully. The three kids are taken away and he and Esteban are awarded certificates. The problem now is that the people of Prairie du Chein do not want that camp with Cuban juveniles in their town. So, the camp is closed and again they have to figure out where to go next. Raphael says there's an opportunity to work with Cuban refugees in Little Rock, Arkansas.

They discuss the possibilities. If the people of Prairie du Chein didn't exactly open their arms to a bunch of Latino people coming to their town and right now they are actually kicking them out, it will likely be the same with the Southerners of Little Rock. Not a good idea.

> *"What if we could write a proposal in San Antonio for a kind of half-way house for Cuban refugees?"* Melissa proposes

> *"Who knows anything about writing a proposal for a half-way house?"*

> *"I know a little."* And he goes on to explain about his work with the VIDA House proposal.

It sounded like a very good idea.

"Now let's get out of Prairie du Chein."

They decide to drive Esteban to Chicago and then go down to San Antonio to line out the idea of the half-way house. Raphael stays behind to make arrangements to close the camp.

Later, in some town along the way, they stop for dinner at a restaurant. Upon entering all conversation comes to an abrupt halt. Everyone stares at the three Mexicans who just walked into the establishment. The three strangers could feel the hatred in the air. The lack of hospitality was palatable. They sit at the nearest table and notice everyone around them is talking and pointing at them. The waiter approaches.

"Yeah, what'll you have?"
"Can we see the menu first?"
"Yeah sure." The waiter replies, very unfriendly.

All eyes are still on them and the tension rises. Finally, Melissa has had enough.

"Waiter! Stop that order, we will not be eating in a place like this! Let's go guys."

The two men follow behind her. They can see Melissa is really pissed off And as they near the door, she stops, turns her head towards the two men and loudly yells.

"I know what you two are thinking on doing. Don't you dare flip off anyone in this RACIST JOINT!"

They get back to the car. Esteban steps on it and they race down the road toward Chicago to find a better place to eat. They'll look for a drive-thru this time.

18

SAN ANTONIO

A fter dropping off Esteban she easily navigates out of the big city like she had been here before. He is totally lost. It's late at night and they check into a motel. In the morning they grab a quick cup of coffee and they're off.

They reach San Antonio by mid-morning and she decides to give him a quick view of the city. He never expected such a beautiful city! Downtown, the Alamo and then a stroll through the River Walk and he is amazed. For breakfast she takes him to the famous *Mi Tierra* restaurant. Everyone speaks Spanish! He notices the Tex-Mex accent from the waiter and she orders for him; fajitas and eggs. Up to that point he had never heard of fajitas. The breakfast was delicious. In the car she tunes into a Spanish-speaking radio station playing Tex-Mex and Mexican music.

"It's local," she says.

He's impressed. It's early 1980 and yet there were no Spanish-speaking radio stations in San Diego. The Mexican music and radio shows were being tuned in from Tijuana.

She now drives to her house.

She lives on Blanco Road. It's a nice three-bedroom home with a big front-and backyard with a tree-lined street and limbs that meet at the top, creating a tunnel. It reminds him of Sacramento. She has two kids she had not told him about. Alicia is 14 and Jr. is 8. He never asked about the kid's father. The kids had been at her mother's all this time. She spends the rest of the day making phone calls and tidying up the house.

In the morning they go to her mothers' house. Driving there he can see that this is a barrio. So much of it reminds him of Sidro. At her mom's house Tex-Mex Spanish is spoken. Melissa's mother welcomes him with open arms. He has no trouble feeling at home here and ends up meeting the whole family. Her brother Ramon is of special interest to him. Ramon doesn't seem to have a job, has a very nice house, good car and is very well dressed. Could he be dealing drugs?

Now he is totally in love with San Antonio! The culture is everywhere, not like in San Diego where the Mexican/Chicano culture is only seen and felt in the barrio. It doesn't take long for him to acclimate and he soon immerses himself in the Tex-Mex lifestyle. He even buys himself a Tejana Stetson cowboy hat. Tejana, Cumbias and old Mexican ballads are heard everywhere he goes. He feels completely at home.

Talk of a half-way house for Cuban refugees comes to a stop. Melissa lands a job with John Hancock Insurance selling policies in the city. She is out a lot and he begins to get bored, so he finds some roofing jobs and gets to work at what he does well. He calls home to tell his wife that he is sending money home. She is very cold on the phone and hangs up on him. But he misses her and his son. Feeling ashamed, he breaks down and cries. One day he calls an old friend from San Ysidro. Chano has family in San Antonio and used to live here. He gives him the number to his cousin Pilar. They meet, and she likes him very much. They start an affair.

Things are not going too well with Melissa and he suspects she is also seeing someone else. Then one day she gets home and he notices a hickey on her neck. He confronts her, and she gives a lame excuse as to how she got it. He doesn't believe her and things get worse. Arguments begin, and he doesn't want to stay with her anymore. In the morning he moves out. He packed one bag with a roofing hatchet, nail pouch, knee pads and some clothes. He feels miserable for having committed such a stupid mistake staying in San Antonio and becomes determined to make it work somehow. He doesn't even have a car. He takes a long walk with no destination in mind and decides to call Melissa's brother Ramon. Ramon picks him up and listens to the problems going on with his sister.

"Es una Mula cuando quiere" (She can be a real mule when she wants to)

"I don't have anywhere to go." He tells Ramon

"You can stay at my place for a while, but I am sure that when my sister finds out you are staying with me, she will give me hell!"

"Thanks, man I really appreciate it."

At Ramon's house the two men get to talking and sure enough the topic of drug-dealing comes up. It turns out his hunch was right. Ramon is dealing large loads of weed from Laredo to Chicago. He thinks to himself, "Is that why she was able to navigate the big windy city so easily?" He tells Ramon his story and offers a proposition to take a load to California. He seems interested.

"I can make a few calls to Sidro and Palm City. I don't have any numbers from Sacramento, but maybe in Sidro I can get some numbers."

"OK but call from a phone booth." Ramon warns him.

He finally reaches Miguel in Palm City.

"Hey Carnal, how you doing?"

"Is that you man? Miguel is surprised to hear his voice.

Where you at? How long have you been gone? Thought you were dead or in jail by now."

"Geez thanks! No man, I'm in San Antonio!" He tells Miguel the short story.

"Tengo Merca," (I've got merchandise).

"Aw shit man, there's some pretty heavy shit going on around here. It's not the same anymore. A lot of people have been offed. Tijuas (Tijuana) is a war zone man; there are full-blown gun battles in the street almost every day with heavy artillery like AR 15s and shit. The newspapers talk about "cartels" or some shit I don't know. There's lots of new people moving in, buying expensive houses in Eastlake." Miguel sounds very scared.

"What the hell is Eastlake?" He asks,

"Very rich houses, that are being built around the hills of Otay Lakes! These new guys are paying cash for those houses and taking over the market here. We hear they're saying that now instead of Chula Vista, Eastlake is the new "Culiacansito." Some of the vatos here have been approached by these new people. They threatened some of the vatos saying if they don't do business with them, they will kill their whole family—crazy shit like that! Even the bank in Sidro was busted for something called "laundering."

"So, you think it's a bad idea to bring in shit from here?"

"A very bad idea. What about your connections in Sacramento? These guys scare me, their shit is real, and I have to watch out for my family. Everyone around here is packing now. You're lucky you got out when you did."

There's that word again – lucky! He thinks to himself and keeps remembering that word.

"OK man, take care of yourself and I'll try to stay in touch."

Looks like "back home" is now a very crazy place. Who are these new guys from Mexico? How are they getting such large loads in? Headlines in the paper told him everything he needed to know.

Customs Man Charged With Letting Pot Cross Border

May 06, 1987|JIM SCHACHTER | Times Staff Writer

A San Diego city parks manager used his part-time job as a U.S. Customs inspector at the San Ysidro border crossing for more than a year to wave through cars and trucks loaded with thousands of pounds of marijuana, federal investigators charged Tuesday.

The graft and drug-smuggling charges against Jose Angel Barron, 40, of San Ysidro are part of a nationwide crackdown—called "Operation Clean Sweep"—aimed at rooting out corruption among U.S. Customs Service agents and officers, Customs officials said.

Customs internal affairs investigators arrested Barron Monday night as he worked in the primary inspection lanes at the border crossing.

The agents, who had conducted on-the-job surveillance of Barron on at least nine other occasions since late February, watched him wave two pickup trucks with camper shells and blacked-out windows through the border gate and into the United States without inspecting them or talking to the drivers, according to an affidavit filed in U.S. District Court.

Drugs Discovered

Agents who followed the trucks to two houses in Chula Vista found that each contained more than 1,000 pounds of marijuana, the affidavit says. Assisted by the Chula Vista Police Department, agents arrested six men and a woman, most of them Mexican citizens, on drug-smuggling charges.

A search late Monday found that Barron had $70,000 in cash in his home and "hundreds of thousands of dollars" more at his parents' home in San Ysidro, Assistant U.S. Atty. Phillip L.B. Halpern said.

Barron, a 21-year city employee, earns about $28,000 annually as an area manager for the city Parks and Recreation Department and about $13,000 annually in his part-time Customs job, officials said. He had worked since

1981 as one of a small number of temporary employees used by Customs to help staff border crossings during peak hours and seasons.

According to the affidavit, investigators secretly photographed the alleged head of the drug ring, Angel Garcia Gutierrez, 32, the owner of a Tijuana karate studio, who was among those arrested; entering Barron's house seven times in the last three months.

'Major Conduit'

Halpern said Barron had served as a "major conduit for drugs entering the U.S." and that the drug-smuggling network he allegedly worked with was "a major, major organization." Investigators were uncertain, however, how much marijuana the alleged smuggling ring had brought into the country or for how long it had operated.

Barron was one of a small number of targets of Operation Clean Sweep, which has been under way for about a year, according to Joseph Cunha, acting regional director of Customs' office of internal affairs in San Diego.

Cunha declined to describe the operation in detail, but said its goal is "to ferret out the small amount of corruption in the Customs Service."

A succession of drug-related corruption cases, either alleged or proven, has dogged the agency over the last several years, even as top Customs officials have helped lead the U.S. government's verbal campaign against official corruption in Mexico and Latin America.

Ex-Inspector Pleads Guilty

In San Diego, former Customs inspector Victor Lopez pleaded guilty last week to charges of drug smuggling, receiving gratuities and filing a false income-tax return. Lopez was charged with taking payoffs to wave vehicles loaded with drugs and contraband cheese through the San Ysidro port of entry.

In December, veteran Customs Special Agent Richard P. Sullivan of Bonita was sentenced to eight years in prison after his conviction by a federal jury on charges of taking payoffs, lying to federal investigators and falsifying credit applications.

The corruption charges against Sullivan were tied to an ongoing investigation of drug smuggling by high-level Customs officials in Florida and Louisiana.

Customs officials insist that there is no evidence of widespread corruption in the agency, which serves on the frontline of the battle to keep drugs and other contraband out of this country. But they acknowledge increasing concern about the agency's vulnerability.

"There is a concern, and there is more of a concern now than there was 5 or 10 years ago," said Allan Rappaport, district director in San Diego. "It's just a fact of life there is so much money involved in the narcotics business that there is a great deal of money that can be thrown at people."

**Pipiolo (on the right) and his brother Arty,
circa 1969 – 1970 photo Courtesy of Sandy Leon**

He remembers "Pipiolo" whom he just called "Pips." In 1977 Pips committed suicide by jumping off the Coronado Bridge, the bridge he helped build as a construction worker. Pips was a tough barrio-bred scrapper, but also a sensitive man with a big smile. He had suffered a motorcycle accident that was very traumatic for him. Before working at the VIDA House he and Pips were always together, doing business or just hanging out partying. Once, Pips confessed to him that the other guys were shunning him because "I would freak them out, with the way I am now." He doesn't believe that Pips was so strange now that he could freak them out that way. He thinks there was something else at work here, that caused him so much trauma and pain that he had to kill himself. He believes it was during these years that were the beginning of the change for the Sidro drug dealers. Looking back, it's obvious to him that it was the pressure from the new people in Tijuana that forced a change in their behavior and how they began to do "business." The loads now coming across the border are astonishing. Again, he asks himself, *how can such big loads get across the border so easily?* These stories would later prove what was so hard for him to imagine.

NEWS

Probe Exposes Corruption Among Customs Agents
June 16, 1987 | JIM SCHACHTER, Times Staff Writer

A sweeping, yearlong crackdown on corruption in the U.S. Customs Service has uncovered serious—though not widespread—drug-related improprieties among border and port inspectors nationwide, a top customs officer said Monday. Code-named "Operation Clean Sweep," the campaign was launched last June on the heels of a widely publicized attack by Customs Commissioner William von Raab on the integrity of law enforcement officials in Mexico.

NEWS

Drugs, Money Add Up to Temptation for Police
December 20, 1988 | JOHN KENDALL, Times Staff Writer

Is it the tip of an iceberg or a minor aberration? Signs of corruption among narcotics law enforcement officers are cropping up from one end of the country to the other: big city cops in New York, Washington and Miami, rural sheriffs in Georgia, a federal prosecutor in Boston and government agents and customs officials in California. No one is certain how widespread the taint may be. No one keeps such statistics.

San Ysidro, now seen as the biggest border crossing in the world, is making millions of dollars for the drug lords. Many people asked how this got started. Who started this hell-hole? Why in our community, Sidro? He remembers how all this happened. He remembers his childhood friends fooling around with weed, selling and getting close to making a lot of money. This is the way that plazas get started.

The Narco-culture

In Mexico, the onset of the drug-trafficking culture began to flourish in the early '80s.

The Narco-culture in Mexico is a subculture that has grown as a result of the strong presence of the various drug cartels throughout Mexico. In the same way that other subcultures around the world are related to crime and drug use (for example the Scottish "Neds" and European "Hooligans" or the American Street ganstas and outlaw bikers), Mexican Narco-culture has developed its own form of dress, music, literature, film, religious beliefs, practices and language (slang) contributing to mainstream fashion in some areas, mainly among the lower-income class and at-risk, uneducated youth. Narco-culture is dynamic in that there are various regional differences within Mexico and among those who participate in it.

Los Tigres del Norte:

"Salieron de San Ysidro procediente de Tijuana traian las llantas del carro repletas de hierba mala" (They left San Ysidro coming from Tijuana with the car tires filled with bad weed)

A **"narco-corrido"** (or *drug ballad*, is a subgenre of the Mexican norteño-corrido (northern ballad). It's a traditional folk music genre from Northern Mexico from which several other genres have evolved. This type of music is heard and produced on both sides of the U.S.-Mexico border that uses an accordion-based polka as a rhythmic base.

The first corridos that focused on drugs have been dated by Juan Ramírez-Pimienta to the 1930s. Early non-Narco corridos go back as far as the Mexican Revolution of 1910 and tell stories of the revolutionary fighters. Music critics have also compared narco-corrido lyrics and style to gangster and Mafioso rap.

Narco-corrido lyrics refer to particular events and include real dates and places.[3] The lyrics tend to condone illegal activities, mainly drug trafficking.

San Diego's first Spanish-speaking radio station did not begin broadcasting programs until August of 1987. There were 17 "X" stations Mexican-licensed broadcasts that "jump" over to San Diego, some could be heard in Los Angeles and Orange County[14]. By then the Latino communities of San Diego were already well entrenched in the Narco-Culture.

This genre of music is the evolution of traditional corrido ballads of the U.S.-Mexico border region, which stemmed from the 16th Century Spanish genre of romance. Among the earliest exponents of narco-corrido music was Los Alegres de Teran, a Norteño music group from Mexico. Beginning with their first record in 1948, "Corrido de Pepito", Los Alegres de Teran were pioneers of norteño style duets singing corridos, rancheras and norteño songs. In the 1980s, Rosalino "Chalino" Sánchez contributed to

---

[14] Los Angeles Times August 11, 1987

narco-corridos. Known throughout Mexico as "El Pelavacas" (Cow Skin Peeler), El Indio (The Indian, from his corrido "El Indio Sánchez"), and "Mi Compa" (My Friend), Chalino was a Mexican immigrant living in Los Angeles. He then began distributing his music for a sale price. His lyrics detailed heartbreak, revolution and socioeconomic issues. Soon he was selling mass copies. Sánchez was murdered in 1992 after a concert in Culiacán. In death, he became a legend and one of the most influential Mexican musicians to emerge from California. He is known throughout Mexico and the United States as El Rey del Corrido (The King of the Corrido).[4]

Various companies, government agencies and individuals have sought to ban Narco-corridos. These attempts include a voluntary radio station blackout in Baja California. Representative Casio Carlos Narváez explained that radio executives did not want to make "people who break the laws of our country into heroes and examples." Former Mexican President Vicente Fox also proposed banning narco-corridos.[5] On the other hand, former Mexican foreign secretary Jorge Castaneda argued "corridos are attempts by Mexican society to come to terms with the world around them...You cannot blame narcocorridos for drug violence. Drug violence is to blame for Narcocorridos".[6]

Narcocorridos and their lyrical content

"La Corona", a **narco-corrido** sung by El Komander

Since music plays an important role and is a major influence in the Narcoculture in Mexico, some songs have been tagged as "anthems" so a ban from airplay was attempted there and in parts of the United States. Another point of narcocorrido distribution has been the Internet, specifically pirated or "bootleg" copies of this music being sold in the "tianguis" or flea markets at affordable prices.

Narcocorridos describe the lives of the poor, destitute, and those who seek power through illegal means. Like hip-hop and rap music, the narcocorridos is popular among Spanish speakers who vary in age, including those unassociated with cartels and gangs. The genre is mainstream in many Spanish-speaking countries, along with the emergence of narco and drug consumption drug cultures. It's now accessible in countries including Guatemala, Honduras, Colombia, Peru and Bolivia.

Narcocorridos and crime
Narcocorrido as a money laundering scheme

In Mexico, parts of South America and some regions of the United States' south border, it's common to hear new artists, mainly in folk radio stations, who are unknown in the music industry and have no previous career or explanation of where they come from. These music groups and singers appear frequently on radio, television and public broadcasts with a strong promotion of their concerts. This happens for a fixed amount of time and just as quickly as they appeared, disappeared from the music scene, or changed their stage name. Such artists are commonly manufactured by producers of dubious origin, who pay payola and have events in order to launder money from drug trafficking, prostitution or other illegal operations.

Violence in narcocorrido industry

Between 2006 and 2008 more than a dozen prominent Mexican musicians, many of them connected to the *narcocorridos* genre, were murdered. The violence came in the midst of the Mexican drug war. Of the most popular killed were Valentín Elizalde and Sergio Gómez, the lead singer of Chicago-based Duranguense band K-Paz de la Sierra. In December 2007 both men were nominated posthumously for Grammy Awards in the banda category. On June 26, 2010, Sergio Vega, known as El Shaka, was gunned down in Sinaloa state, shot dead only hours after he had denied reports of his own murder.[23] Ramiro Caro, Gerardo Ortiz's manager and cousin, was also killed when Ortiz's Chevy Suburban was attacked by armed men in an attempt to kill Ortiz, who escaped unhurt.[24]

Other murdered music industry figures include Javier Morales Gómez (a singer for Los Implacables del Norte), four members of Tecno Banda Fugaz, four members of Los Padrinos de la Sierra, Zayda Peña (a singer for Zayda Y Los Culpables) and many others.[25][26][27]

While few if any arrests have been made in these cases, experts and musicians say the murders can be explained by their proximity to drug traffickers.[28] Some speculate the killings could be related to romantic disputes and jealousy.[29] Others cite cases in which a musician has written a song praising or criticizing a drug trafficker. Many assert that Valentín Elizalde's murder for example, was related to his song, "A Mis Enemigos," which some interpreted as an attack on the Gulf Cartel following its appearance in a widespread YouTube video.[30]

There has been debate about motives behind the killings and whether or not the media has exaggerated the trend. Narcocorrido expert Elijah Wald has disputed the assumption that any of the murders were related or that musicians as a whole are targets for drug traffickers.[31] However, given the grisly nature of the murders, some of which were accompanied by torture and disfigurement, few[who?] doubt that drug cartel hitmen are to blame.

In the wake of the high-profile murders of Elizalde and Gómez, among others, some prominent corrido musicians postponed concert dates in certain parts of Mexico.[32] Narcocorrido singers travel with relative ease and security inside the United States, but many Mexican-American narcocorrido singers take extra precautions while venturing into Mexico by hiring extra security, traveling in well-guarded caravans, play smaller venues, and limit their tours into high crime cities in Mexico. Others have said they are afraid to sing narcocorridos in public for fear of offending the wrong person.[28] Likewise, some vendors of narcocorrido CDs have reported low sales, citing fear among listeners of buying a CD featuring songs favoring one group of traffickers over another.[28] This fear, once thought to be silly and paranoid, has become real as Mexico has become the most dangerous country not only for journalists, but anyone who speaks up or is affiliated with the opposing cartel. The Zetas cartel has been known to torture and kill online and social media bloggers who speak about them. In one incident, the tortured and mutilated bodies of a man and a woman who had posted about cartels on social media were found hanging off a bridge in the city of Nuevo León, in September 2011. A sign stating, "This is going to happen to all the Internet busybodies," was found next to them and signed with the letter Z.[33]

Growing popularity in the United States

Recently, much of the new narco corridos music is being aimed directly at the American Market and produced mainly by Mexican-American entrepreneurs. Like many other concerts or sporting events, many corrido artists are choosing American cities as venues for the ability to fill the concert halls at higher ticket prices than would be affordable by the average Mexican citizen. Many of the music and CDs are distributed by American labels as well as videos, intended specifically to be sold in the United States.

The growing popularity of the music in the U.S. is correlated with Mexican immigration. Over a quarter of the residents of the Los Angeles area are now Mexican and they have brought this folk music style with them. Narcocorridos are now played in L.A. clubs, on radio stations, and do not have the negative stigma attached to them in Mexico as they once did. This is mainly because the Spanish lyrics are only understood by Hispanophones, and the distance American society has with the reality of Mexico makes them feel they are only listening to works of art and fiction.[34] [15]

The Polleros also seem to have free territory to ply their own disgusting trade and are now making thousands of dollars through Sidro. He knows Raul through a mutual friend. He is a pollero asking to sell him four kilos of weed. It's a small buy and he must deliver the goods himself. He has never seen how the polleros operate and he takes Randy along for company and protection. They drive to the apartments on Broadway near Palomar Street and across from where the Target is now located. He tells Randy that he will go in alone because they would be very uncomfortable with a tall long-haired white-guy in their apartment.

---

[15] Wikipedia

"Stay here with the weed, I won't be long," he tells Randy.

He goes in and pleasantries are exchanged. He makes the mistake of asking Raul how business is doing.

> *"Uuy muy bien Carnal, ahorita tengo gente que va a traer $400 cada uno! Ven veras"* (Real good brother, right now I have people in there that will get me $400 a head. Let me show you.")

Raul takes him into one of the bedrooms. He sees about 12 people including five women and seven men crammed into the bedroom; some on two beds, the others on the floor leaning on the walls.

> *"Que te parece?"* What do you think?

He just shakes his head slowly not saying anything.

> *"Mira, esa morrita en la cama, esta muy buena, si quieres nomas ve y llebatela al otro cuarto - de mi parte, claro!"* (See that young girl on the bed, she is fine! If you want her, just go over there and take her to the other room, on me of course!")

> *"Sabes que? No puedo, vamos por the mota, y a que me pagues"* (You know what? I can't, let's just go and get the weed so you can pay me, and I'll leave.)

They walk back to the car and Randy hands him the four kilos. He gets paid and they leave.

> *"Hey man, you alright? You don't seem so happy. You mad or did something go wrong in there?"*

> *"Fucking Polleros disgust me! How can they be making money like that? Fucking exploiting their own people! Fucking low-life, I'm never doing business with those motherfuckers again!"*

19

HOMELESS IN SAN ANTONIO

I t was a bad idea, for a load trip to California. Ramon takes him room-hunting on Broadway near Breckenridge Park where they find a shady looking, run-down motel to rent a room. The roofing jobs have stopped offering so he goes to work for a tool outfit, selling them out of a pick-up in nearby towns. That job doesn't pan out as he hoped. Pilar comes over a couple of times but is soon disappointed at the way he is now living and stops coming over.

By the end of the third month he can't afford to pay the rent and is locked out of his room. His meager belongings are confiscated for the time being. He spends the night on the floor in his neighbor's room. He's broke and learns there is a blood donor office nearby, so he goes there and sells a pint of his blood for $14. He can eat for that day. He calls his mom to ask her to send him some money and realizes he's at an all-time low. He had never done that before. She sends him $70 through Western Union and there is some relief. This will at least get him his tools back from the land lady and a couple of nights to sleep somewhere. He won't be able to sell another pint of blood until two weeks have passed.

Now it's gotten so bad he must sleep in the park with old newspapers to cover him. One night he is sitting at a bus stop bench and a woman passes him, stops, looks back and comes over to him.

"Want a date?"
"No thanks, I've got no money."
"Where you from honey?"
"San Diego."
"Cheez, you along way from home, huh?'
"Yeah."
"Have you eaten anything today?"
"No not today."
"Here sweetie. I don't ever do something like this, but I've had a good night tonight, I'm a whore you know."
"Yeah I know."

She gives him $10 and leaves. He runs over to the nearby Chinese restaurant and orders a rice and chicken bowl. Reflecting on his bad situation, he looks back at all the money and opportunity he had in his past life. He could have had a degree, even a master's from Stanford and he would not be in this miserable hole now; lonely, broke and homeless. The regrets are tearing at his heart—his wife, his son! Lamenting, he recalls the mistakes. By now the Vision Quest wagon train must be well into its trek to Arizona. How he wishes he was out in the wilderness acting like Davy Crocket, not here alone broke, on a park bench. How he wishes he had at least his guitar to hold in his arms, to strum and play some old tunes. He remembers as a teenager how he would fall asleep caressing the curves of his guitar. He covers up with some old newspaper and falls asleep on the park bench.

The next morning, he spots a new construction project that is ready for the roofing phase. He asks for a job as a roofing shingler.

"Just give me a chance to show you what I can do, I can give you 15, maybe 17 squares a day!" (Each square is 100 square feet of roofing space)

"OK we'll see. Get on that loaded section over there. All the material is there already."

He gets to work hand-nailing shingles and the boss goes up on the roof where he is working.

"You got good hands kid, keep going."

He does 12 squares that day. He is out of shape and practice. The boss is paying $6 per square, so it is a good day. The next day, he notices an ole' boy on the roof next to him. He has a whole different system for shingling, not the California style. The man is watching him. At lunch time he introduces himself as Clyde. He's in his late 50s or so.

"Man, I saw your shingling; you are not from around here are you?"
"No, I'm from California, San Diego."
"How long you been shingling?"
"Oh, off and on since I was 18."

During break and after work that day, Clyde keeps up with the questions, so he tells Clyde his situation and recent history.

"Want to team up?" Clyde asks.
"Yeah sure."
"OK, why don't you come over to the house and as soon as you get paid here at the end of the week, we can go and look for a place for you to stay closer to my house, wadda ya say?"
"Yeah sure!"

Clyde lives near the Lackland Airforce base, way on the other side of San Antonio with his wife, two sons and two daughters. Clyde's wife doesn't seem very happy to have a new person at the house, but Clyde is the boss here so she puts up with him at least for a couple of days. At the end of the week they find him an apartment nearby. Clyde comes to pick him up in the morning. He's driving a new red Toyota Mini-pickup, great for the roofing jobs that are now more regular.

Things are going well, but change does come soon. Clyde's eldest son has accepted a new job in San Jose, California and Clyde's wife is going with her son, taking her family along. Clyde is not going and insists that they go on ahead. Timmy, his teenage son wants to stay with his dad. Clyde's family moves out, while Clyde, Timmy and Rusty, their red lab dog, stay behind. Clyde decides to set up camp at the local KOA campgrounds. Clyde invites him to leave the apartment and come stay with them in the tent. It's a large 6-person tent and Clyde has all the extra equipment. Three guys and a dog; two white guys and a Chicano live in that tent

The work is off and on, sometimes not for a while. On one occasion they have nothing to eat.

> *"You know that those ducks down at the river over there look like they might be good eating. Why don't you two boys go down to the river and snatch up a couple of fat ones. The ducks are not afraid of people, just take this bread here, feed them and snatch them as they are eating,"* Clyde says.

The boys just look at each other. *He is serious huh?* So, they go down to the river where there aren't very many people around and grab two ducks. They had to hold their beaks to quiet them down. When they get back to camp Clyde already has the hatchet and chopping block on the picnic table. He proceeds to chop off the head of each duck and hands one to each boy.

> *"OK begin plucking the feathers. Each of you gets a plastic bag. Don't let the feathers fly all over the place. It's against the law to kill ducks in public parks,"* he says with a wink and a smile.

Clyde then cleaned, gutted and roasted the ducks in his barbeque. The ducks tasted OK, a little chewy, but the meal of roasted duck with roasted pecans was delicious. The campgrounds are full of tall, beautiful Pecan trees. The next morning, they found work.

At around 4:30 a.m. Rusty is barking like all hell broke loose and as they're awakened, they hear clanking and noises. Clyde runs out and finds a tow truck taking his Toyota away. Clyde runs and manages to climb into the driver side and he, the Toyota and tow truck are off!

> *"What the hell was all that about?"*

"The bank has repossessed the truck; Dad has not paid his monthly bill on it for months. I don't know how they even found the truck! Somebody must have told the bank where they could find it."

He remembers Robin.

A short time later they see the tow truck coming back to camp. The two are happy to see this thinking that Clyde had talked the driver into giving him his truck back. But as it makes the turn, they can see Clyde still sitting in the driver's side. They begin to laugh at the sight but see that Clyde is not laughing. He has his head down, arms across his chest, looking pissed off and worried. The tow truck stops in front of the tent and Clyde begins to unload their roofing tools.

"Come on goddammit, stop staring at me and come help unload the tools. Shit, shit, shit!" he yells.

"What happened?"

"The fucking driver didn't know I was in the truck. I was hoping it would become unhitched as I hit the brakes whenever we hit some of the speed bumps and I could drive away but he noticed me down the road and stopped to get me off. I asked him to please at least let me keep my tools. Now what the fuck are we going to do?"

They had food and some money to last a few days, but that was not enough. Clyde decides to call his son in San Jose to come and pick them up he but can't come for them in at least another month. If he came right away, he would be in danger of losing his new job. But he's able to send some money to hold them through. The plan was that they were to take him along and drop him off in San Diego, then drive up to San Jose. They could have just left him there to try and make it out on his own, but he was very touched to hear Clyde insist that they would take him home. Of course, it would cost them a lot more in gas, but Clyde insisted and would not leave his friend behind.

In late November, Clyde's son arrives at the camp, just in time to avoid the winter weather. They quickly break camp, pack up the Ford Station wagon and head out. On the way he calls his mother and asks her to call his sister and tell her he is on his way. He tells her that three friends will drop him off and asked if she could please have something to eat for them since they have done him such a great favor to get him home. As they leave San Antonio he looks back and thinks what just 10 short months in San Antonio had cost him and all the city took from his life. But he also had some take-aways. He didn't know just yet until someone in San Diego pointed it out, but he brought back some of that Tejano/Tex-Mex accent in his voice along with the priceless bitter life experiences.

On Thanksgiving Day, they arrive in the early afternoon at his sister's house in City Heights. His sister is preparing the Thanksgiving dinner. He is not a religious man, but he is so thankful to his sister, Clyde and his sons for delivering him back home that he almost breaks down and cries. He's able to hold it back but Clyde can see his emotion, smiles at him and tells him that he "knows." His sister serves them a great helping of turkey with all the fixings. Later he bides them farewell, sure he will never again see them again.

20

PALOMAR MOUNTAIN

From his sister's house he calls his wife. She doesn't sound all that happy to have him back but relents. She is still staying with her mom and they need to find a place to live again. He keeps roofing for a while because he is still very wary of going back into the weed and coke business. He is out at night now more often trying to make ends meet and gets in trouble twice for driving under the influence. Each time he spends the night in jail. This is not working out and he is desperate to try something else.

By sheer luck an old roofing buddy Ray, who he had met on a big job in Mission Viejo, calls him saying that he's been living on the La Jolla Indian Reservation on Mt. Palomar. There's a small two-bedroom house for rent right up the hill from him. He's collecting unemployment insurance from his old roofing jobs. Ray says it only costs $75 per month but water and gas must be brought in from outside. It does have electricity though, and a new friend Matt from the "Rez" would likely help him out with the water issue.

There is now a warrant for his arrest in San Diego due to failing to appear in court for the DUI's and he needs to get out of town again.

It's October 1981 and they go up to Palomar to see the house. From there he can see a big pasteur with cows and to the right of it is what he learns is the mushroom factory. He loves it! From the highway it's a short drive up the dirt road to the house where he sees a big front yard overgrown with weeds, a small fenced garden, and pen with a shed for animals. Inside he spots two propane tanks, the kitchen has a stove and refrigerator and in the living room there's an old pot-bellied stove that also works as a heater. "*But what about the bathroom?*" his wife asks. There is no need for showers or bathrooms since there is no water. Then from the window he sees the outhouse and they will need to use the nearby campground called "Oak Knolls" for showering. He hadn't thought or asked Ray about that issue. Will his wife and son live this way?

They load up the old pickup that he had just replaced the motor on and they're off to the mountain. Ray is there to meet the new neighbors and he introduces Matt, a "real Indian from the Rez." They help him move in and they all seem to get along. Its late fall and there's a big need for firewood. He would have to get a good chainsaw to cut wood for heating, so he cuts a good pile of logs from the surrounding woods. At night they hear coyotes nearby and realize he needs to get a dog. He goes to the pound in Escondido and adopts a beautiful one-year-old German shepherd who he will call Sam. Then on a drive through Valley Center he spots a sign that someone is giving away two Afghan hounds. He stops by the farmhouse and picks up the dogs. They are also very beautiful; one black and one blonde with long fur and fangs. The owner tells him that Afghans are very hard to train, almost like cats—they will be loyal and stay if fed and treated right, but don't try and teach them any tricks. He will call one David and the black one will be Goliath. No more worrying about coyotes. The dogs get to mark their territory quickly and sleep under the house for the time being. The Indians on the Rez call the Afghans monkey dogs. Matt tells him, "*Some of the people are afraid of those dogs.*"

The outhouse stinks badly. He must dig another hole and move the small shed. He completes the job faster than he imagined, fills the hole with dirt from the new one. Now he must clear the front yard. Matt advises him that with a couple of goats the yard could be cleaned up quickly. He tells him that his uncle Clyde has goats he's selling cheap. He buys the two goats from Clyde and names them Cheech and Chong. The goats do the job in two days, during which time he fixes up the pen where Cheech and Chong will sleep. The dogs and goats get along and spend time playing around the yard. He's happy at what he's done so far. He begins to clear the garden. Winter is coming, and he hopes he's prepared the family for the coming cold.

As the animals acclimate to their new home, he begins to take them on short trips around the property to see how well he can control them with just his voice. They escort him and his son down to the bus stop. There they go, him and his son, Sam, the two Afghans and the kids Cheech and Chong. What a sight they make. After a few days he wants to try something new so as they're going by the old oak tree, he stops, and Sam turns to see why. He yells, "Go Sam go!" and waves his hand for them to keep going. Sam takes the lead the Afghans flank him, and the kids are jumping around. When they get to the bus stop the dogs sit and wait. His son gets on the bus, the animals turn around and go back home. They meet him at the oak tree. *"Good Boy Sam!"* He pets all of them, even the goats.

Winter is nearing and one day as he is heading out to the woods to collect the firewood, he'd cut the day before, the dogs are silently following. As they come to a clearing, he spots a deer. "Meat!" he thinks, "It's a doe." He steadies the dogs and whispers, "Down, Sam." Sam lies down with his paws in front of him and the Afghans do the same. He is carrying his 9-millimeter pistol, a Taurus semiautomatic with a 14-round clip and one in the chamber. If he could get a few rounds into her the dogs would take care of the rest, but if he only gets one in and she runs off the dogs would not catch up to her and she would die of the wound or coyotes would finish her off. He is aiming at the animal but at the last minute he can't pull the trigger, feeling sorry for the doe. *"She probably has some little Bambi somewhere hidden in the woods"* he thinks to himself. He also realizes the dogs are not firearm trained anyway. The deer gets to live.

That winter it snowed regularly, but Matt tells him he has seen worse. It is such a beautiful sight out of their window. The old pot-belly stove does a good job of heating up the house and they make it through the winter with no problems.

However, the unemployment insurance isn't working out and he needs to work for cash. One day he spots a farmer down in the valley who is building a large shed or barn of some sort. He goes down to talk him into letting him do the roof. The shed is 20 squares, or 200 square feet and they agree on $8 per square for the job. He completes the job in a day and a half and the farmer is amazed he could finish so soon. Still worried about their finances he asks Matt about a possible market for weed.

> *"Oh yeah everybody smokes weed around here, but very few have any money. The campers always want weed though! What you should do is get that garden going and plant yourself a few primo seeds."*

He makes plans for a garden and around the perimeter he will plant corn to hide the young marijuana plants, some tomatoes, zucchini, and whatever else will fit into it. The garden is roughly 17X8 feet with plenty of space. Its early fall and the plants should be blooming by May. During this time, not very many people were "home growing" marijuana and law enforcement were not yet using aircrafts to spot illegal plots of land, but soon that would change.

The next generation of growers of homegrown marijuana began experimenting with new strains to create more potent, cross-bred plants. It was widely considered that these new strains were mostly brought to the states from Amsterdam. To better control the environment the new seedlings were brought indoors. Soon it was discovered that special lighting was required so they experimented with incandescent lighting and later after much trial and error a new High Intensity Discharge bulb was used, which helped produced a more potent strain of marijuana.

HID lighting was first used by large warehouses. For start-up and smaller companies, HID lighting is not very cost-effective, so certain light companies began to realize that there was a huge demand for a smaller device and began perfecting the efficiency and size of the bulbs for indoor plant growing. This was done under the guise of allowing the public to grow their own vegetables in their homes, when in reality the marketing of this equipment was really aimed at underground marijuana cultivation.

The potency and quality of marijuana products grown indoors was improved and perfected several times-fold, thus, producing large amounts of money that would eventually lead to the growers and business people of the still illegal weed to become less dependent upon the southern Mexico drug cartels.

In the early 2000s' the cartels reacted to the competition and actually brought people from Mexico to produce what was to be called "Guerrilla Growing." The cartel growers would plant the new seedling in the middle of national parks and open land, mainly in central California. It produced hundreds of pounds of weed not as potent as the California weed grown indoors but it would sell at a better price than the traditional weed coming from the cartel fields throughout Mexico.

The cartels began funding "front men" starting in California and other states that legalized marijuana. It seemed as weed became more legal the future for illegal weed was less profitable.

The trade began in what is called the "Emerald Triangle" in Humboldt, Mendocino and Trinity counties, started mostly by white college students who were studying agriculture. Then the practice was passed down to apprentices and secret cliques that were highly guarded. By then the price for a pound went up to $5,000. Broken down into ounces and grams, the weed could fetch up to $60 for one-eighth of an ounce. At this rate one could make anywhere from $6,400 to $6,700.

He prepares the animal pen for chickens and to protect from hawks he adds a roof. Soon he has a nice-looking farm. The dogs and goats keep the chickens safe from hawks and coyotes. Things are looking well for the little homestead and there is plenty to eat. The animals are healthy, and the chickens are producing eggs. His wife is soon pregnant.

21

THE LA JOLLA INDIAN CAMPGROUNDS

The campgrounds to the people of the tribe are a major source of income. All who live on "the Rez" must contribute some of their time to helping with campground maintenance and any other duties that may be needed. The campground is about two miles long and snakes alongside the San Luis Rey River, nestled into a beautiful wooded valley. Matt tells him:

> "We just call it "the river." Yeah if you live on the Rez you get free electricity and water, so we're expected to put in our fair share of the labor."

> "Yeah of course count me in. What kind of work?" he asks.

> "Stuff like emptying the trashcans from the campsites, picking up litter; sometimes I work the gate, but I don't think they'll have you doing that. Right now, they are getting ready for the annual round-up next month. Can you ride a horse?"

> "Oh yeah," he says with a smile. "Man I was raised under a thoroughbred horse's ass! I'd love to go on that round-up!"

> "Thoroughbreds huh? When was the last time you were up on a horse?"

"Man, it's been a few years."

"Well if the elders choose you to go; you will definitely get a very sore ass after the first day."

He's not selected to go on the roundup and instead is asked to help with stocking the river with fish. He travels with the men in two flat-bed pickups, each carrying two big water containers. They are going to Lake Henshaw to load the fish. They pull up close to the big release valves and with a sturdy net catch the fish as they come out, throwing back the smaller, undesirable fish. Once satisfied with the catch they drive down to a selected area upstream from the campground and begin to unload the fish into the river.

"Grab yourself a fat one for dinner tonight," one of the men tells him.

"Oh yeah, my wife would like that," he says as he grabs a fat bass and stashes it in his pouch.

By now Matt has introduced him to most of his family and friends on the Rez. Clyde is his uncle and one of the elders. Clyde likes to drink, sometimes too much. One-night, at the house, Clyde gets so drunk he passes out in the shed on some bales of hay, Clyde is not there in the morning, he must have stumbled down to his house.

After an argument with his wife about his heavy drinking she is fed up. The next morning, she asks to take her to her mother's house for a while. She wants a break from the outdoor life. So, he drives her down to her mom's house in Del Sol, a good hour and a half drive. Immediately, he goes back up the mountain.

It's spring now and his garden is beginning to look nice. The plants are about four feet tall by now and the buds glisten like amber in the sun. He wonders how he and Matt are going to sell the weed.

"We'll get a couple of Clyde's horses and ride up the river looking for some rowdy white-boys. They are sure to buy a lid or two." Matt tells him.

"What about the people of the tribe? Won't they know? And what could they do to us?"

"Naw man, the people don't mind if it's only weed, just don't try and sell the hard shit. That could be enough to get you kicked off the Rez. They want happy campers, and if they are high on weed, that means more business for the camp store. We just need to be very cool, don't make any scenes."

The river is full of campers this season and the plants are ready for harvest. They cut enough buds to make around 10 lids. They've smoked a few joints before and know its good weed. Matt advises him:

"We'll ride to the river tomorrow, real slow; I know who we are looking for. You have to look like a real Indian! Don't wear the hat, get a bandana, wear a ponytail, and shave. Not too many Indians can grow a beard like that! He jokes.

The next morning, they saddle up at Clyde's farm and ride to the river. They enter the campgrounds at the southwest end and slowly come up to the campsites. Matt looks around and nods over to a campsite. They approach slowly. Sure enough, there is a white teenager looking at them and comes over.

"Hey man, are you guys real Indians?

Matt looks down at the kid from his horse, palm up and does the "HOW!" thing.

"Far-out man! Hey, you guys want a beer?"

"Yeah OK." says Matt.

They come down from the horses, and walk over to their campsite, accept a beer and make small talk. Soon enough the white kid is asking;

"You guys wouldn't know where we could get some grass or even a joint, would you?"

"Got any money?" asks Matt

"Yeah we've got money."

There are six young adults in that camp, guys ranging from 17 to 19 years old. Matt pulls out a joint and hands it to the kid and the kid passes it around to his friends.

"Man, this is good shit! Can we get a few or even a lid? How much?"

"I'll make you guys a good deal, just because you are camping out here and doing business with the tribe. Just for you guys we can sell you a lid for $90, they usually go for $120."

"OK man we'll take two lids. Can you guys do two at that price?"

Matt reaches into the saddle bag and pulls out two lids and takes the money. They saddle up and go to the next camp with the same routine as the first one. They sell all 10 lids that day. It's a good day. They ride back to Clyde's farm, unsaddle and return the horses to their pen. He gives Matt his take, one-third of the profit. Matt is happy.

22

ARRESTED AT THE REZ

His wife miscarries the baby and troubles begin. His old gut feelings come back about her lies and he thinks to himself, *"Why couldn't she carry this baby to full-term? Why could she carry their son and not this baby?"* He is full of tormenting doubt. She didn't even tell him the baby's gender. He drinks more now. He and Clyde have all-nighters in the shed and arguments between the couple escalate. One night they're both shouting at each other and she starts throwing things around the house. He grabs her and shakes her to stop. *"Fuck it! I'm going to sleep."* She sleeps on the couch that night.

In the morning he is lying in bed extremely hung-over. No one is home. The pickup is gone, and then suddenly the dogs start barking. He hears cars coming up the hill. He looks out the window and sees two patrol cars approaching the house. As they stop in the driveway, he hears his name being called from the patrol car speakers.

> *"We need for you to come out at once and put your dogs away or we will be forced to shoot them."*

He comes out and orders the dogs under the house. They obey, and an officer handcuffs him.

"We have a warrant for your arrest for failure to appear in court over a DUI violation."

The officer puts him in the patrol car and they drive off. He can't believe what is happening! Did his wife turn him in? She must have told them how to get to the house! As they reach the highway he turns around and sees his dogs following the patrol car until they reach the highway.

He is taken to the downtown county jail where he will stay until his court hearing. He's got no chance of bailing out because he is a "flight risk." At his hearing he's sentenced to 17 days at the Descanso County Camp. After a few days in jail he's boarded on a bus to Descanso, a labor camp up in the hills of the East County. At the camp he's given a bunk to share with another inmate.

The work is hard and consists of clearing brush and weeds and cutting firebreaks. He gets along with no problems and soon it's time for his release. They give him his clothes and the $50 he had with him when he was arrested. The first thing he does is call Matt from a phone booth.

"Hey man, she told us everything—how she had to turn you in because of the drunken asshole you've been. And she tells me that you will not be coming back to the Rez again."

"What about the dogs and my animals?

"She cleared out everything in the house, sold off the animals; I don't know what she did with the dogs. There is nothing left in the garden. She took all the plants, just pulled them right up."

"Shit that pisses me off!"

Next, he calls his mother, asking her to take him in for a few days.

"Eres mi hijo, te quiero mucho, ven a la casa." (You are my son I love you, come home now.) He takes the bus to his mom's house and tries to settle

down. Of course, his mom knows the whole story, but she will never side against him. His mom knows more than she tells him about his wife.

That night he goes to a friend's house and gets very drunk. He decides to go to his mother-in-law's house to speak with his wife. When he arrives, the argument starts all over. Her brothers are with some friends in the house and they come out to see what's going on when somebody "cold-cocks" him and he goes down in the front yard. He comes to with a policeman shaking him to get up. He is cuffed and placed in the patrol car.

> *"No charges have been filed against you, but you will have to spend the night in jail for drunkenness."*

> *"Officer, I think my jaw is busted."*

> *"We'll have the doc look at it over at the jail."*

On the way to jail his head feels like it will explode. His face is starting to swell. He is still plenty drunk.

> *"You big pendejo! Just this morning you are released from jail and here you go again back to jail and it is not even 11 p.m. yet!"*

At the jail the medic checks him out and gives orders that he must be taken to the hospital. The doctor at the emergency room tells him his jaw is broken.

> *"We will have to perform surgery on your face. We see that it was broken some time before, right?"*

> *"Yeah, a couple of years ago."*

> *"Man, you're going to have to learn how to duck or something! If we're lucky we won't have to rebuild your jaw, but for sure if you come in again with a broken jaw we will have to and that will not be a pretty scene, plus it will hurt like hell."*

The doctors wire his mouth shut again. He wakes to find surgery scars around his neck. They tell him they had to "open him up" to be able to put everything back in place. The next day he is released from the hospital and his compadre Julian is there to pick him up. He won't have the wires removed for 11 weeks and he needs to heal up.

Following the incident, he has several conversations with his mother. She understands and suggests that he go to Texas and work with his brothers in the oil fields of Amarillo. He agrees and makes plans to go to Texas again.

He remembers San Antonio and the hardship he endured there. This is yet a much harder blow to his life. He lost all that which was very dear to him—a home he worked so hard to build, his animals, his wife and son.

The 11 weeks of healing wore on in a boorish and painful agony. The weekly visit to have his wires tightened got to be routine, he knew what to expect. Then one day at the hospital, just as he is heading out the door, he runs into her again. There she was, like an angel with open arms, beckoning him. *Its "Little Egypt!"* His high school sweetheart, the one who broke his heart so many years ago:

> *He came from somewhere back in her long ago,*
> *The sentimental fool don't see*
> *Tryin' hard to recreate*
> *What had yet to be created once in her life*
> *She musters up a smile for his nostalgic tale*
> *Never coming near what he wanted to say*
> *Only to realize it never really was*
> *But what a fool believes, he sees*
> *No wise man has the power to reason away*
> *What seems to be*
> *Is always better than nothing*
> *Than nothing at all.*[16]

---

[16] Doobie Brothers 1978

23

AMARILLO, TEXAS

lmost 17 years had passed since they last saw one another and the reunion ignited a hot love affair—they couldn't wait to get their hands on each other. The same afternoon his mouth is unwired she invites him over to her place of business, and right there on the floor of the back room she engages him for sex. The following week he had to fly to Amarillo, so they made sure to make the most of every day. He learns over time that she is a very astute business woman and he admires that about her. She's done very well for herself and it shows with a large two-story home with a pool in the suburbs of San Carlos, a new Pontiac Trans-Am with all the "bells and whistles" and of course the constant bundle of cash she carried around.

After he leaves for Amarillo they stay in touch daily. At the airport his brother Tury picks him up in a Chevy Monte Carlo. He's got a nice two-bedroom apartment where his wife and child used to stay. He doesn't bother to ask his brother about what went wrong with the marriage. Their younger brother *Catchito,* who they just call "Katch" now, comes over with his wife and child. They celebrate their coming together and talk about the older brother's turn to roughneck in the oil fields.

There is no problem getting the job and soon all three brothers are working the same rig from 3 to 11 p.m. It's physically hard work, especially in mid-December when it's cold, sleety and snowy.

Then one night the accident that was waiting to happen, happened. Tury is up on *"the monkey board"* half way up tower where the next section of pipe that needs to be connected is lifted, and as usual with the two other brothers down on the rig floor. Katch suddenly hears Tury screaming but it's hard to make out what he's saying since the big diesel motors are so loud. Katch tells the operator to stop the motors and Tury comes down with his hand all bloodied and a shocked look on his face. They take him into the *"dog house,"* which is what they called the oil rig shed next to the platform. Tury's left thumb is missing. The operator calls the Medics and Katch is told that he needs to climb up the tower and look for the missing thumb, he goes up and returns holding Tury's thumb with something coming out of the other end. A helicopter is called to come pick him up. That was the end of Tury's roughneck career, as well as that of his two brothers.

Meanwhile, daily conversations are still happening with his lover in San Diego and she tells him that very soon she will be driving up to meet him. He's excited about seeing her again but still unemployed and without a vehicle. They plan to meet in Lubbock, Texas.

On the agreed upon day and time she picks him up at the bus station. He's happy and aroused when he sees her again and she too is excited. She had already rented a motel room and they quickly made up for lost time. The next morning they headed for Amarillo. His brother welcomes her.

> *"So, what are we going to be doing for a whole week?"* she asks with that sexy smile.

> *"Want to go horseback riding?"*

> *"Yeah, but I have never been on a horse before!"*

> *"Don't worry I'll teach you."*

> *"Where are we going to ride?"*

> *"Palo Duro Canyon."*

"Are you serious? Hard Stick? Is that the real name of the place or are you just joking with me?

They all laugh because "Hard Stick" is a Spanish euphemism for "hard penis." His brother had taken him to this beautiful canyon before, and remembers he had spotted some horse rental stables and made the plan. The next morning, they headed out for Palo Duro Canyon. With that sexy giggle of hers she says, *"Yes! I want to go see that Hard Penis place!"*

She is totally is amazed at the beauty of the huge canyon.

Palo Duro Canyon is the second largest canyon in North America after the Grand Canyon. It's carved out over the geologic eons by the Prairie Dog Town Fork of the Red River. Its 120 miles long, 1,000 feet deep, up to 20 miles wide. Crossed by numerous breaks, washes, arroyos, and side canyons, it's a force to be reckoned with.[17]

On the horse his lover has no trouble learning to ride, but at only 5 feet, 2 inches tall she needs help with the stirrups and adjustments. Once saddled in, he is proud of the way she handles herself—no fear, only excitement. During the ride they take in the spectacular scenery and he notices that she seems almost sexually aroused when she quickly proves his hunch right. She spots a small clearing under a tree.

"Help me get off, rubbing back and forth on this saddle is getting me very excited, wanna do it here?" she asks.

He knows it's not only the saddle, this place would bring out an erotic feeling to anyone, he thought. The whole area is deserted. Eagles, hawks and jack rabbits are their only witnesses.

They make love there under that tree, and then get right back to more spectacular sightseeing until it's time to go back to the stables, ending the most wonderful outing they ever had. On the way home, she asks him to

---

[17] From *"Empire of the Summer Moon, Quanah Parker and the RISE and FALL of the COMANCHES, the most POWERFUL INDIAN tribe in American History.* Copyright 2010, by S. C. Gwynne

stop at an "Ice House" she spotted on the way in. *"Please stop there, I want to get a Popsicle,"* she said. He found it a little odd since he's never known her to eat a Popsicle before, but he obliges. She waits until he's back on the highway to open it. She then unzips his pants and begins to rub him, takes a big bite of the Popsicle, throws the rest out of the window and begins to give him oral sex. He had never felt a sensation like that before. *"Where does she learn all this shit?"* he asks himself.

Back at home the three brothers are still unemployed. Mike, a neighbor of theirs who lives with his wife and daughter and is a friend of Tury's, tells him there will be temporary work re-piping at the gas plant where he works. The gig pays $9 an hour and could provide for about four months work. Tury is still disabled, but Katch and he will take the new job as soon as it's ready in two weeks. It looks like *Little Egypt* also brought good luck to Amarillo.

At the end of the week she needs to get back to San Diego and she easily convinces him to help drive her back in that badass Pontiac Trans Am. She would pay for his ticket back to Amarillo. The weather is bad through the Texas panhandle and they decide to stop off in Albuquerque, New Mexico to spend the night. The next day the weather is better. Several times when they would pass big-rigs the drivers would see her fooling around with him and blow their horns, doing fist pumps and *"woohooing"* as they drove past, laughing. One trucker went a bit too far when he keep catching up to them to get a better look, then yells out his window,

> *"Hey baby, show me your tits!"* This pisses him off enough to give the finger to the trucker. *"Fuck you, asshole!"*

He slams down the gas pedal of the Trans Am, the tires squeal and the car fishtails leaving the big-rig far behind. *"Fucking redneck, now you can go jack-off that slimy thing of yours on down the road!"*

Back in Amarillo he calls her, and she tells him to look in his closet for a Christmas present she left him. Inside the box he finds a beautiful pair of Tony Lama cowboy boots. When he goes to try them on, he finds an envelope with two one-hundred-dollar bills! He feels so humbled, realizing he can't give her anything back. On the phone she says, *"You gave me the best week I have ever had!"* He takes the $200 and uses half of it as a down payment on a truck he's had his eye on for some time. It's a 1972 red-orange Chevy pick-up, which for being 7 years old had low-mileage and motor that hummed. With the new job coming he's sure he can pay it off and then some.

The job at the natural gas plant is all about rerouting a pipeline for a new building. The plant sits in the middle of an open prairie where on the site there are silo-like buildings, aluminum sheds, and big farm-like sheds with pipe lines leading everywhere. There are six laborers on the job. Bob Sr. is the boss of the welding company that has been contracted to perform the operation. He and his son Bobby will do the welding and pipefitting when the ditches are ready. Daily, he sees Bob spending a lot of time just watching the crew work. Then one day after about a month on the job, Bob calls him into the shed.

> *"Can you drive a tractor, like the one over yonder?"* Bob points to a tractor that's been parked there for a while. He remembers Willey's ranch.
>
> *"Yessir, learned how to drive one of those back when I was 9 years old."*
>
> *"Good, you 'fraid a heights, are you?"* Bob asks him
>
> *"No sir, been a roofer now about 10 years."*
>
> *"Very good! My company is going to get an ongoing contract to finish this new job, I'll need one man to scatter sand with the tractor and also to do some high-beam work to insulate pipe, you up for it? Pays $9.50 an hour."*
>
> *"Yessir, thank you sir!"*

After the ditch-digging the rest of the crew is laid off and he begins his new duties. He gets well-adjusted and looks forward to coming to work every day. Mike is also on the job as a permanent pipe insulator and teaches him all he knows. They become great friends.

> *"Hear ya going to be doing some high work, huh?"* Mike asks. *"Pretty scary shit up there. Ya gonna be working over two big ol' turbine engines that make a lot of noise. Anyone who falls into them will end up in pieces man! Ya gotta be careful!"*

On the first day on the job it's about 4:30 p.m., when Bob calls out to them.

> *"Ya 'all come down from there now, put the tools away, it's time to go to da house."* He turns to Mike and asks, *"Are we going over to Bob's house?"* Mike laughs and says, *"man, he means its quittin' time, we are done for the day."*

He'd never heard that saying before. When he worked with the crew there were set hours for work and quitting time. He gets the "high work" done strapped to a safety line, satisfying all the plant bosses almost daily while he is up there.

"Hell of a good job son!" Bob tells him at the end of the job, which almost takes a week to complete.

The job lasts through the spring and he is happy. On one of his weekends off he flies back to San Diego. During a stop over in Albuquerque, two young ladies come to his seat.

> *"Do you mind sitting in between us?"*

> *"No not at all."*

He gets up to let them squeeze by. He smells their perfume and notices how beautiful both Chicana women are. He soon finds out their names are Genie and Virgie and they are in their mid-20s. They turn to him and begin small talk. He learns they're on their way to Las Vegas while their husbands are off "on *their silly hunting trip.*"

"They let us come to Vegas for the weekend to be bad!" Virgie says. Shortly thereafter Virgie begins to touch his leg, and then begins rubbing it. Genie asks where he's going, and he tells them of his girl in San Diego. Genie disregards his admission and asks if he wants to go with them to Las Vegas:

> *"I'd love to, but my girl is waiting for me at the airport and we are very excited about seeing each other again."* He tells both,

> *"She must be very special for you to turn down two chicks, to stay with the whole weekend,"* Virgie says.

> *"Yes, she is very special."*

Once they land in Las Vegas Virgie plants a kiss on his cheek and slips him her phone number.

> *"If you're ever in Albuquerque again give me a call,"* she says.

When he arrives her brother is there at the airport to pick him up.

> *"Sis is over at the shop waiting for you. She asked me to pick you up because she can't leave the shop alone."*

When they arrive she's at the counter looking as beautiful as ever in a cowboy hat. He looks around and sees the shop is decorated in Western theme. She named it *"The Wagon Wheel Shoe Repair Shop."*

They spend a great weekend together and on Sunday morning he is scheduled for an 11:30 a.m. flight to Amarillo. They leave early for the airport and she decides to stop off at Presidio Park in Old Town San Diego. They take a stroll through the woods and she finds a spot where they have sex—an occurrence that will be repeated frequently in the future. It wasn't the most discrete place as passersby would spot them making love from time to time, but they'd just giggle on past.

Back in Amarillo and back to work at the gas plant, he begins driving a tractor that scatters sand evenly over the newly-laid underground pipeline. As he lowers the tractor bucket he starts at one end and backs up, bumping the bucket in reverse to spread the sand level. Later he must go back and rake it.

It was a good job and he learned much of the operation of a natural gas plant and a sense of where the entire pipe goes and what they do. But it does come to an end. There are other short-term jobs at other plants that Bob contracts with, but they also come to an end. He goes back to roofing. On a cold, rainy day he is sent out on a steep roof job. He arrives and is amazed to see two men in the sleety rain laying wood shingles. He thinks to himself, *"They've gotta be nuts to be up there in this weather!"* They keep their footing with two-by-four boards nailed to the roof.

"Ok, if they can do it, so can I."

He gets his gear and ladder from the pickup and begins on his side of the big house. At lunch time they introduce themselves. Jose and Pedro are Kickapoo Indians and they travel with their families all over the panhandle of Texas looking for roofing jobs. The trio soon becomes friends and Jose and Pedro invite him to their apartment to drink beer and introduce him to their family. Everybody joins in on the drinking. There's a lot of laughter, food and stories. He notices in some of the children signs of what appear to be Fetal Alcohol Syndrome but doesn't say anything. They stay friends for several more jobs and then one day they tell him it's time for them to move on.

During one of his lover's trips to Amarillo to visit him she insists on tagging along to a roofing job. She tells him how amazed she is at the speed, in which he nails shingles, flashes that sexy smile and says, *"That turns me on! If it wasn't so hot up here, I would do you on this roof!"*

During the last trip she'll make to Amarillo, he takes her to the zoo and tells her, *"Yeah, not much to do here in Amarillo."* Near the summer of 1982 they agree it's time to leave Amarillo and she says she will teach him all there is to know about working her shop. His younger brother Katch had already left for San Diego and Tury would stay for a while completing his rehabilitation and insuring his disability status with the state. On the last day he packs up the Chevy, says farewell to his brother and to Mike and his family, and he is off to San Diego.

The next day he begins his apprenticeship at the shop. He learns quickly and with a master shoe maker doing the resoling he is soon able to manage the shop by himself. He provides excellent customer service, making loyal patrons out of the customers. Being bilingual helped the shop immensely, his lover does speak some Spanish, but not as fluent as him, and once word got out to the Latino community, that there is a Spanish speaker at the shop business began to boom. At the end of the evening he would have two shopping carts full of men's and women's shoes to re-heel and resole.

After five years the shop is well known. Dick, the accountant, began pitching them a proposal to start a board and care facility for folks suffering from Alzheimer's disease. Dick convinces the couple that good money can be made in this business. They can sell the shop while they are searching for a suitable house. Dick had done his research well and easily convinces them to sell the shop and buy a large house he's seen in El Cajon. He will write the proposal to the County of San Diego for a major use permit and sign up with the California Association of Rehabilitation Facilities for membership. Training to become certified nurse's assistants or CNAs, would take 11 weeks to complete and there was also six months of mandatory hands-on experience working at local board and care facilities to be completed beforehand.

In order to make monthly payments at the new house they would have to rent out rooms and space for "men only." The house is a beautiful ranch-style home and has a second 3-bedroom home, with property that sits atop a knoll with a private road leading up to the gate. It overlooks the valley at the intersection of Los Coche's Road and old Interstate 8. The facility would be named Rainbow Hill. Things are set into motion; the shop is sold, and they begin to move into the new house. They divide up the large master bedroom with single bed spaces and in total, including the guest home; they have rooms for 11 renters. It rents out to full capacity in short time.

He moves into the house and goes back to roofing to cover personal expenses. At the beginning things are going well. Dick is working on the permits but then begins to take too much time. He has trouble with the men at the house. Dick is gay, and the renters don't like it when he comes around. Problems also begin when women start coming over to the house and they have drunken pool parties and eventually sex with the men. Dick has had enough and quits. He tries to do the permits himself but issues at the house continue. One morning he wakes up to find Little Egypt straddling on top of his chest with his old .25 caliber pistol starring him in the face, this after finding out he'd been sleeping with another woman. He easily grabs the gun from her hand and throws it out the open window. *"Would she really have pulled the trigger?"* he asks himself. Later he goes out to the yard to retrieve the gun and finds it empty of ammo. They talk and are able to reconcile.

> *"But I want all the renter's out of the house! I will pay the monthly mortgage from the money received from the shop and you will continue roofing to pay your part."*

Slowly he begins evicting renters. The guest house now has a whole family living in it and they stay. When the main house is empty, she moves in with him again. At this point he has a young roofing apprentice named Jorge helping him out on jobs. Jorge doesn't speak English and he can see that she is attracted to Jorge. This makes him angry all the time, and he begins to drink a lot. Arguments become more frequent until she moves out. He can't make the mortgage payments with his roofing salary. On the roof he tells Jorge about his problems and Jorge suggests they go back to his home town in Mexico – Culiacan Sinaloa. Jorge is a boxer and says they can make money in Mexico by taking advantage of his boxing skills. He tells him he could be his manager, something he knows nothing about.

They agree to meet in Mexicali, but it gets late and Jorge still hasn't called so he goes to the bar where he and Jorge had met before. He gets so drunk he falls off the barstool. Around 3:30 in the morning he wakes up in his mini truck in the passenger seat. His face hurts so he looks in the mirror and discovers a swollen eye. As he looks around, he notices he's not wearing his zip-up boots. He finds them zipped up and tucked into the corner in front of him. "What happened last night?" He tries to remember but can't. He obviously blacked out. He notices a street vendor at the corner and asks him if he saw him get into the pickup last night, or if he saw a fight. The vendor either didn't see anything or doesn't want to say anything.

He drives back to his cousin's house confused but suspicious. When he gets there, he opens his suitcase and finds his .357 pistol missing. Everything else is in its place. He tries harder to remember what happened last night. He thinks, *"Who, but a shoemaker would handle shoes in such a careful manner?"* In the morning he goes to Jorge's sisters' house and she tells him that Jorge and the lady with her son had just left. His suspicions were proved true. They left him in the truck last night.

He has nothing left to do but go back to San Diego. Unfaithfulness on both sides ended the relationship. Back home, his mother is now living in Encinitas with her new husband Hector. She became a widow some years ago when pop had a heart attack and died in the back of a horse van. He was only 47 years old. With no where to stay he will sleep in a trailer that Hector has parked in his front yard, until things get better. In a couple of days his cousin calls telling him he has just saw Jorge and his ex-lover at a bar in Mexicali.

> *"Agui podemos chingar a los dos, si quieres." (Here we can do both of them if you want).* "No, no les hagas nada! dejalos, ya paso todo." *(No, don't do anything to them. Leave them alone, everything has passed now.)* He orders his cousin to let them be.

With his self-esteem at an all time low, he feels ashamed, saddened, betrayed and at one time just worthless. He needs to find a job that will put him back together again. Too broke to buy roofing tools he finds a job painting houses with a friend of a friend.

24

"A REGULAR JOB"

An opportunity appears. Rachel, a barrio sister from the Chicano Movement and is the director of the Barrio Station, which needs a program coordinator for a new program called Project STAR. He goes to the interview and is surprised that Rachel hires him on the spot.

He begins the job in earnest, daily traveling from Leucadia to Barrio Logan. Soon a new sense of self-esteem begins to emerge, and life is now more fulfilling. He comfortably settles into the new job, providing supervision to a staff of six counselors in a very challenging environment. But the work suits him well and he is good at it. As Rachel once told him, *"You wrote the book on Project STAR."*

The Sidro drug-dealers begin to get more cliquish and less trusting of people they have known most of their lives who are, now not allowed in their inner circle. They are moving bigger loads, making more money and buying and renting ranch-style homes in Bonita. When Pips kills himself, he's shocked. Never would he have thought that his dear friend would do such a thing. He remembers Pips back to his Little League days, later hanging and partying with him and the vatos at Bea and Freddy's house.

As coordinator of a youth-gang intervention program funded by the city, called Project STAR (Street Alternatives and Resources). Below is an excerpt from ***An Informational Aid to Undersstanding Gangs, Groups, Cults,*** by The San Diego County Deputy Sheriffs" Association 1990.

The Barrio Station, a nonprofit organization provides a wide array of gang and drug diversion services to Black, Chicano and Asian youth in the Southeast communities of Logan Heights, Linda Vista, Golden Hill, and operates through grants and city funding. The project deters youth from gang and drug involvement and redirects potentially violent gang activities into wholesome, law abiding ones. The program, which has three black counselors and three Chicano counselors, that work with youth gangs, ages 13 to 22 years old and has seven satellite offices throughout these communities in the City of San Diego. Each counselor was assigned a caseload of 200-plus youth".

Executive Director: Rachel Ortiz
Coordinator for Project STAR: Juan Medina

He had a staff of six experienced counselors assigned to local gangs to provide resources, serve as role models and ideally pull the kids completely out of the gang environment. During his time as coordinator they frequently found themselves at the site of drive-by shootings. He remembers one incident at St. Jude's Catholic Church during the annual bazaar they were alerted to a shooting just around the corner. He and his counselors ran to the scene to find two teenagers lying in the street. One had been shot in the chest with what appeared to be a 380-caliber bullet. He could see the slug lodged in this teenager's chest. The other boy he later learned had died by a shot fired from a 22-caliber weapon. A young mother came to the office asking for help in cashing out her son's pay check from "The Hire-a-Youth Summer Jobs Program" to help pay for her son's burial. The boy was simply in the wrong place, at the wrong time.

Soon he hears of "La eMe" the Mexican Mafia. Many eMe members were being released from prison and back into their communities. While in prison they had made connections with Mexican drug cartel members and the time was ripe for recruitment of soldiers for The Felix Arellano Cartel in Tijuana. There is now a serious recruitment effort of young 30th Street gang members by ex-cons of La eMe. They are taking these kids to Tijuana to be trained assassins for the cartel. The violence is widespread in Mexico and he begins to hear in the news of captured and killed cartel members with familiar gang monikers. He sees pictures in the papers and remembers those kids from the Barrio Station's recreation room. They were just innocent teenagers getting into a life that would destroy themselves and their families.

He now has a management position in workforce development programs in the community. During that July of 1995 he learns that his compadre Julian was killed; a shot through the neck while sitting in his car at a McDonald's in Chula Vista. He had been with some other guy. It's still unknown who that other guy was. They said he was messing with someone else's woman. Was this really "rage killing" over a woman? He has doubts about that. Could this be a planned assassination for territory? Knowing Julian as well as he did, he knew his compadre would not budge for anyone. At that time Julian was doing very well, he had a big ranch style house in Bonita and drove a 211 Porsche. He and his associate had a well-established landscaping business that served as a perfect front for his other business of moving large loads of weed. Julian's murder is now a different story to him. This must have been the beginning of the change Miguel was talking about. That big change had everything to do with the TJ Cartel and other cartels in an epic battle for the coveted Tijuana–San Ysidro Plaza territory.

More than a year later a new job opportunity arises at the Urban Corps of San Diego. One night after work, Sam the director, pitches the job to him over beers at Chuy's Bar in Barrio Logan. The Urban Corps of San Diego is a program funded by the California Conservation Corps as well as county contracts. The organization hires low-income, inner-city youth who are at-risk of juvenile delinquency. Their job is to do things such as highway litter clean-up and county parks trail/pathways building, among other things. He is offered the job of coordinating a recycling program. He tells Sam that night to give him three weeks to submit his resignation at the Barrio Station. Rachel is not too happy but graciously accepts his resignation.

The work at Urban Corps is rewarding and he proudly wears the brown uniform of coordinator. It provides the opportunity for program staff to counsel, guide and be a role-model to corps members for integration into a more productive, crime-free way of life.

By April of 1992 another job opportunity comes his way. Occupational Training Services, Inc. has just been awarded a grant from the San Diego

Workforce Partnership to operate the Hire-A-Youth Program. It's a summer job program for low-income, gang-affiliated youth. With his background he's offered the position of program manager. It's a $2.6 million contract that includes subcontracting with programs like the United Pan-Asian Communities and two community-based, youth gang diversion programs. He has a staff of 15 in satellite offices throughout the incorporated communities of the City of San Diego. His "summers" begin in April of each year and end in October. Work includes staff recruitment and training, setting up and supplying the satellite offices and job development at government and non-profit agency sites to provide work experience for the youth workers between 14 and 18 years old. In May and June recruitment and eligibility certification of youth begin the season for the summer youth jobs program.

He will complete six summers of the program at OTS (Occupational Training Services). He's learned the strategies involved in grant and proposal writing and has teamed up with a teacher from the San Diego County Office of Educations' Juvenile Court and Community Schools to write the grant for court schools. Now with a strong resume of youth service provision they are awarded the contract for the 1997 summer youth program.

His service to the community will blossom as he is awarded the Certified Workforce Development Professional with an endorsement in Management Services and go on to work with adults. The last 10 years of his career were spent working in supported employment for adults with serious mental illnesses. He is now supervising Master's level employee's.

Not a bad resume for someone without a college degree.

Despite all this, he still feels a need to cruise the streets of Sidro. He drives to the park behind the Civic Center, remembers playing tops with the kids, stealing eggs from Lupe, the milkman's truck, playing in the hills. He drives by all the houses the family had lived in, there are no longer any horse ranches in town, only along Monument Road, and these ranches all have different names now. The old library is now a museum, Larsen Field, our little league field is now a County park, with a recreation center and grassy areas with picnic tables, the old fire station is now a beauty salon and a music shop, where he took guitar lessons, at one time. He stops by the *San Ysidro Feed & Grain* store to chat with Tommy.

> *"You're the one I sold my black '72 Cadillac to, right"*
>
> *"Yeah, wish I still had that 2-door beauty"*
>
> *"Let me show you something,"* Tommy fumbles around the grain barrels. *"This old grain scoop is one of my treasures; you know how I got it? Your Pop's gave it to me, many years ago; I will never part with it."*

By 1996 he is with his new fiancé at the house of a long-time friend of his moms.' She is giving his fiancé advice.

> *"El es un gran hombre, pero a tenido muy mala suerte con malas mujeres, hubo un tiempo que hasta yo lo queria para mi hija! Estoy segura que le vas hacer una buena mujer."* (He is a great man but has had very bad luck with women. There was a time when I wanted him for my daughter. I am sure that you will be a good woman for him.)

After 20 years of faithful marriage, he is happily married to that skinny little girl he certainly passed by all those years ago in the Zocalo of that beautiful city Oaxaca. She is Elsita.

As he looks back and recalls that if four major events would have played out in his life, he would not be in the position he now finds himself: One. He would be dead, could have happened on several occasions. Two: Prison, lengthy prison terms were handed out in those days for even small amounts of weed or cocaine. Three: Vietnam. If he had not changed his draft status in 1969, he would have gone to war, returning with a severe case of PTSD or killed in action. Four: With a Masters Degree from Stanford University, he would surely be doing fieldwork in Anthropology somewhere in Mexico or Latin America. This final option is the one he regrets the most.

> *(Because I was so much older then, I'm younger then that now.)*

The End

ACKNOWLEDGEMENTS

To my loving wife Elsita, for mustering up the courage to support me in this project. I can only imagine the shock her Southern Mexican family will have when they find out she married an ex-drug dealer, despite all of it being behind me. To my mother, Carolina, may she rest in peace, who taught me the meaning of respect, integrity, commitment to the community, and the importance of helping those less fortunate than yourself.

To my son Ariel, who laughed with me throughout this project and inspired me to keep pursuing this book. With his help I truly believe that a better writer and human being emerged, there is no greater blessing than a father and his adult son laughing together. To my other son Juanito, who is autistic (non-verbal) and was my patient shadow. The tragedy of losing a daughter, victim of domestic violence, that left my wife and me, as parents to our two little grandkids, Romina 9, and Nadxieli 7. Tragedy also brings many blessings, these two little ones are a true blessing I thank them for giving me the space to stay on track. Losing their mother, Rocio Duncan in the horrible way that she died, is a great challenge to our family. To our other kids, my step-kids; Jorgito and his wife Gretel Agapito, Monse and our great-grandchildren, Ainne, the beautiful twins Carito, and Vickie (mi Vippy).

To my editor and dear friend Allison K. Sampite, who very tirelessly used her professional know-how to make the manuscript come alive. I need to mention Joseph Wambagh, my conversations with him, when I first started this manuscript gave me the push I needed. *"Juan, this your story, no one needs to read it, for you to pursue your goal, I'm an old geezer now, I will be glad to see it published"*. After re-reading his book **Lines and Shadows**, I decided to go forward on this project.

To The Friends of San Ysidro that meets monthly at the Family House restaurant in National City and is managed by my old friend and elementary school classmate Oscar Parra, also a hell of a lefty pitcher in the San Ysidro Little League "The Toros."

To Newton Phillips, who without his encouragement and *"Follow your dream"* encouragement, this book would still be in limbo. To Richard Medina who (no relation) gave me the most valuable information to continue with this project. He put it very well when he said that the *"vatos de Sidro"* were not only the *"enablers"* for how the Mexican cartels were able to take over the Tijuana-San Ysidro plaza but made it clear that the U.S. government corruption had a bigger role to play in this drama when compared to some Barrio kids. To Sandie Leon, Pipiolo's (and my little sister) thank you *"hermanita"* for the pictures, and the encouraging words. My *"Comadre"* Doris Carlock, my compadre Julian's widowed wife. Doris, thank you for the conversations and the heads-up on much of the history that you have so neatly tucked away in that beautiful head of yours.

To Jackie Gechter, another classmate and Sidro neighbor, who now to me is the unofficial historian of San Ysidro. One can spot *"El Jackie de Sidro"* at any given time cruising the streets of Sidro looking for ways to better our community. To Tommy Cuen, who still runs the *San Ysidro Feed and Grain* store. I remember the Cuen family like they were my own. His brother Conie, may he rest in peace, was like my big brother as Tommy was.

To Francisco (Paco) and Elvia Medina, They carry the same last name, and we love like family. They have cheered me on, through many nights of laughs together.

And finally, to my old friend Jose Barron, who collaborated with me at the onset of this project. He suggested the title for this book. Thank you, *mi amigo*.

The San Ysidro family has a very deep-rooted pride and perseverance in keeping the memories alive. Georgie (George Miranda) *Guero* (Juan Michaels), Clarence Arroyo, (may he rest in peace), Ralphy (Ralf Lopez), Carlos Mercado, whose images appear on the front cover of this book, will always be my very loved brothers *"de Sidro!"*

CPSIA information can be obtained
at www.ICGtesting.com
Printed in the USA
JSHW032216230522
26110JS00003B/192